Sergeants Ruth & Flora

Sergeants Ruth & Flora

An American & an English Woman Serving in
the Serbian Army During the First World War

Nation at Bay

Ruth S. Farnam

An English Woman-Sergeant
in the Serbian Army

Flora Sandes

LEONAUR

Sergeants Ruth & Flora
An American & an English Woman Serving in the Serbian Army
During the First World War
Nation at Bay
by Ruth S. Farnam
An English Woman-Sergeant in the Serbian Army
by Flora Sandes

FIRST EDITION

First published under the titles
Nation at Bay
and
An English Woman-Sergeant in the Serbian Army

Leonaur is an imprint
of Oakpast Ltd

ISBN: 978-1-78282-423-7 (hardcover)
ISBN: 978-1-78282-424-4 (softcover)

http://www.leonaur.com

Publisher's Notes

The views expressed in this book are not necessarily
those of the publisher.

Contents

Nation at Bay

RUTH S. FARNAM

Contents

TO THE
DEVOTED WORKERS
WHO LIVED AND SUFFERED
AND DIED IN SERBIA

PHOTOGRAPH USED BY THE AUTHOR
ON PASSPORTS

Preface

My readers will see why I cannot send this little book forth without at least craving their indulgence. Since it is my first book it will doubtless have many faults but in it I have tried to express the deep emotions, the admiration and the respect which the sight of Serbia's great courage has aroused in me; the experiences that I have had in that beautiful, suffering country and, above all, to pay tribute to the noble men and women of England, France and America who volunteered to work among those unhappy people. Men and women who served unfalteringly amidst the most deadly dangers and who, in many cases, laid down their lives while aiding those Serbian heroes who themselves counted life as naught when sacrificed for flag and country. Because my whole heart is in this book I offer it to a generous pblic with the hope that it may increase the awakening interest in our splendidly brave and devoted ally, Serbia.

The Author   Madame Grouitch

Convalescents at Madame Grouitch's Hospital in Belgrade, 1918

Chapter 1

A Backward Glance

We Americans as a nation have never exhibited a great deal of interest in European affairs. One might say that we were almost provincial in this regard, isolated, as we are, by the vast expanse of ocean. To many of us Europe has been regarded merely as a place to visit for pleasure or business.

Such places as Serbia and the other Balkan States were of no more interest to us than Siberia or Arabia. We heard of them seldom, except when they were at war. And the impression prevailed that these "half-civilized" countries spent most of their time fighting with one another.

We were so wrapped up in our own affairs that we had no place in our thoughts for those distant lands. But we forgot that our horizon was rapidly enlarging. The fast ocean steamers, the cables, the expansion of our foreign trade—all these things were quickly bringing the far-off peoples closer to us. And the time came almost before we knew it when the internal affairs of almost every country in the world affected us in some vital way.

Yet even after the outbreak of the European War we still felt that we had no national interest in it—that we were not affected—that it was none of our affair. In fact it was only after repeated insults and actual acts of war committed against us that we reluctantly consented to enter the conflict. Perhaps the bungling German intrigue in Mexico and Japan did more toward awakening us to our peril than anything else.

When Austria declared war on Serbia on July 28, 1914, it was at Germany's bidding—and Germany reckoned on a great world conflagration as the outcome. She had played the game of political chess over and over again in secret, with Austria, Turkey and Bulgaria as the pawns, and she had proved to her satisfaction that she could win the game when the time came to play it in public.

The United States was taken into consideration—just as surely as was France, Russia and England—before the ultimatum was delivered to Serbia. And yet we went about our affairs entirely unaware of any plan to include us in the great game of world domination. Who in America in July, 1914 could foresee that the result of the first shot fired on Serbia would be the sending of millions of our own boys to Europe—even to Serbia—to save civilization?

And now that we are in it to a successful conclusion, having joined hands with all the other countries fighting Germany and her accomplices, we are becoming intimately acquainted with all of our Allies. We are meeting even the less-known ones in their own homes, so to speak, and are beginning to feel that they are real human beings like ourselves, whose acquaintanceship we are sorry we had not, cultivated long ago.

Serbia, whom we may have at one time charged with starting the war, now appears to us in a different light altogether. By a backward glance at Serbia we may learn for ourselves a little about the peculiar sequence of events which culminated in this war—and get a few new glimpses of a history which has been to us hitherto either utterly unknown or merely a half-told tale.

Many years have elapsed since the Austro-Hungarian Government began to trade upon the innate loyalty of the Serb. When Turkey rolled her hordes over the famous Field of Kosovo in 1389, and overwhelmed the Serbian armies, taking possession of the land and crushing Christianity under her iron rule, the Serbs looked to Austria as a nation of fellow-Christians for aid. This aid Austria pretended she would give while she was for centuries really fostering ill feeling between the Balkan Slavs and Russia, thinking thus to increase her own influence and bring under her Empire all of the Serbians, many of whom had already settled in Austria-Hungary.

Jealousy of Russia and greed of extended power were her motives for assuming a friendly mask toward the Serbs. But she did not hesitate to cast this mask aside as soon as it suited her to do so. After many years of oppression of her own Slav subjects, she began an active policy of annexation and one after another Bosnia, Croatia, Herzegovina and Dalmatia were obliged to bow to her rule. Having a secret understanding with King Milan of Serbia, she plotted to destroy Russia's influence in the Balkans and soon succeeded in rousing Bulgaria to defy her great protector, Russia, whom the only half-educated Bulgarian politicians suspected of wishing to hold their country as a Province.

Prince Alexander of Battenberg, who had been placed on the throne of the new Kingdom of Bulgaria, began to plan for the union of divided Bulgaria, whereupon the Serbian King, Milan, immediately declared war upon him. Thus Austria's well laid plot had succeeded. She was able to play off one country against the other to her own advantage; her ambition being to gain more territory in the direction of Salonika, or even perhaps to possess that part of Macedonia in its entirety. As this war resulted disastrously for King Milan, he appealed to Austria, who intervened and exacted a fearful price. This price was a secret allegiance whereby King Alexander, Milan's son and successor, became entirely a tool of Austria.

The Serbians now found their ancient Constitution set aside and Teutonic influence rampant in the land—for we must not forget that in recent years Prussia has always been behind the central European intrigues. The people murmured, and struggled to disengage themselves from the octopus-like tentacles which were strangling them. Their effort at last culminated in the terrible tragedy at Belgrade in June, 1903, when the unhappy Alexander and his wife, Draga, met their doom at the hands of a few stern and uncompromising men, who had been driven to desperation by the sight of their country's impending ruin.

Under the rule of the new King, Peter Karageorgevitch, who was placed on the throne after the death of Alexander, Serbia began to recover herself, and her devoted people to know once more the advantages of liberty and the blessings of at least some measure of peace. Schools began to spring up in the villages, and manufactures of many kinds flourished; but jealous Austria, malignant Turkey and treacherous Bulgaria lay ever in wait at her gates.

Then in 1912 came the war with Turkey. After this Austria prepared to attack Serbia, and only postponed doing so because of her inability to secure the consent and co-operation of Italy. But Bulgaria, thirsting for revenge because she had not received what she considered her share of the spoils in Macedonia and secretly abetted by Austria-Hungary, attacked the little nation and, it is needless to say, was well thrashed for her pains.

By this time Serbia was fully awake to her danger. She sharpened her sword, she filled her munition depots, collected stores and equipped her armies. She could see looming before her a great war, waged by the three countries which were bent on her extermination. Dauntless and ready, facing these enemies, many times her own size, brave Serbia stood—a Nation at Bay.

In July 1914 the expected attack came. How she fought in this war, which since then has embroiled practically the entire world; how she fought and won again, then for a time lay helpless under the lash of a pestilence, shunned in that dark hour by her enemies, then rose to her feet weak and tottering again gallantly to face the foe; how the traitor, Bulgaria, came slinking to share the spoils, and how devoted Serbia fought and strove, calling vainly for the western Allies to come to her aid; how at last these friends prevailed upon her army to evacuate the beloved country that it could no longer hold—to take refuge under the wings of these Allies until its awful wounds could be bound up and its starving soldiers fed, rearmed and reclothed that they might return by a new route and fight again for the freedom and honour of Serbia—this story of courage and sacrifice, of suffering and devotion, will fill many pages of history for future generations.

My own country is now at war with Germany and Austria and though I am a member of the Royal Serbian Army I am also a true American. I know what our boys will have to face and I know, too, that they are as brave as any other soldiers of the Allied Nations—and now they have the opportunity to prove it. They will face a cruel, cunning, desperate foe—and they will conquer and drive him back— yes, back to Berlin. Worthy of our highest traditions will our army prove itself. Worthy of that flag which we all love—the flag on which the stripes represent our national honour, which has never yet been stained. Those crimson bands which were dyed a deeper red by our fathers' blood on the battlefield: while that field of midnight blue— not so dark, alas! as the night of pain which now prevails in Europe— holds the shining stars of our national ideals.

Today, (1918), there can be no such word as "pacifist." We are at war. Men and women who live under the protection of the American flag and claim the privileges of American citizenship can be only one of two things—Patriot or Traitor! That we should uphold our Government in its effort to bring this war to a speedy and successful conclusion, that we should each one of us do our share cheerfully and gladly to that end: that we should avoid destructive criticism, placing ourselves at the disposal of our great Chief Executive as the indispensable cogs of the great machine of State—this is our clear and bounden duty.

If we Americans, each and all, do our duty soon it will be no longer heroic Serbia who is "The Nation at Bay" but "Germany at Bay!" May we so wage this, our war, as to prove by sword and Right that as our fathers fought for our freedom so shall we fight until the Blonde Beast Prussia is finally crushed and the world set free forever.

★★★★★★

In this little book I have tried to tell something of the small part I played in this great fight; how I, a stranger, knowing little of the country and less of its people, was impressed by its heroism and devotion and was finally caught up in the whirl of its magnificent struggle against the evils which my own country now is prepared to attack.

CHAPTER 2

My First Introduction to War in Serbia

"It reminds me," I said, "a little of Naples with the beggars lying about in the sunshine."

"There are no beggars here," replied Madame Grouitch. "These are sick soldiers, just back from the war, and there is no place in the city where they can be taken in."

On leaving the station in Belgrade, I saw numbers of men in their dust-coloured rags, sitting on the steps or lying on the ground under the trees. In my ignorance I had mistaken them for beggars. A broiling sun poured its rays down on them, and sometimes a man would moan and feebly roll over to gain the welcome shade of a stunted tree. I was told that at night the carts would go around and gather up the dead. Every hospital was full to overflowing and nearly every house had as its honoured guests, sick and wounded soldiers.

This was in August, 1913. I had been in Serbia before, during the Turkish war, and when I received an invitation at this time to come to Belgrade to see the return of the victorious Serbian Army after defeating Bulgaria in the Second Balkan War, I went gladly.

Madame Grouitch, who is a charming American woman from Virginia and the wife of a Serbian diplomat, was doing marvellous work for her adopted country. Unable to bear the thought of these heroic men exposed to such suffering, after their splendid campaign, she went to the government and demanded that one of the school buildings be turned over to her during the vacation. In this large school she founded an auxiliary hospital, which was called "The 22nd Reserve Hospital." She went to the merchants and townspeople and asked for beds and other furnishings. Then she had the sick and dying men gathered up and laid on these beds, under a roof for the first time in many months.

Because the people of Belgrade had previously given nearly all they had, the fitting out of this hospital was of the crudest description. The beds on which the fevered soldiers lay were simply the iron frames with three pieces of board laid across. On this comfortless foundation were placed large sacks filled with straw. Smaller sacks formed the hard pillows.

There was no bed linen and no clean clothing. In the city there was a college, in which young orphan girls from every part of Serbia were being trained as teachers. So we sent up there and to the extent of our funds, we got sheets and pillow cases, of coarse cotton, and shirts and drawers for the men..

These garments served a double purpose since they could be used first as hospital clothing and later when a man left the hospital he had only to add the heavy socks and untanned leather sandals, a home-spun waistcoat and wide girdle to be completely clad in the peasant manner.

One day a large bag was brought into the "Gymnasium," one of the wards, and its contents dumped on the floor. There were about a dozen garments in the heap and it was hard to tell which were coats and which trousers, they were so ragged and worn. All were stiff with dirt and great blackish stains of blood. Clean-edged cuts of bayonet thrusts were there and jagged holes told of more terrible wounds. Not a garment was fit for use.

One boy of twenty looked at a particularly shapeless rag and said cheerfully, "Yes, that was my coat. Luckily I will only need two-thirds of it anyway, now." His right arm was gone!

It was very hot and there was a glare of light from the high un-curtained windows and the flies were so awful that the men could only sleep by burying their faces in the hard, hot pillows. Most of the younger men, however, were apparently as cheerful as if they had no care in the world; but some of the older ones lay patiently, day after day, looking at us with great hopeless eyes that pierced our hearts. Many had lost an arm or a leg and their minds could only ponder on how their wives and families were to live and bear this extra burden. Serbian families are as a rule very large and the people are very poor, and all mast work hard, so a maimed man knows himself to be a sad drag.

But no man uttered one word of complaint and none regretted

his sacrifice for Mother Serbia. Their gratitude for anything we could do for them was touching, though they were absolutely frank in their comments.

One day, under the tuition of a young Serbian orderly, I made Turkish coffee for the men. They are very fond of it and will drink large quantities of the syrupy stuff. When the little cups had been drained, I proudly asked, "Was it good?"—thinking to be commended.

"Not very," came the reply. It was several days before a chorus of "*Dobro*," (Good) rewarded my efforts and they seemed really pleased for my sake that they could at last approve.

We had only the coarsest food, in most cases only rather dry bread, and occasionally a vegetable stew, but as long as we could supply them with cigarettes, almost the breath of life to the Serbian soldier, they were contented.

When I had been in Belgrade two days, the Red Cross unit which had been serving in the hospital, was withdrawn and shortly after sailed for England. This left Madame Grouitch with two trained nurses, Dr. Shuler, a young English surgeon who had gone to the Balkans to gain experience before settling down to practice, two Serbian medical students, and a number of ladies and young girls, belonging to Belgrade society, but with little training (as we understand it), to care for one hundred and sixty-eight men, most of them suffering from neglected and gangrenous wounds. Madame Grouitch was herself so worn out with her unremitting efforts in the hospital that she nearly broke down.

However, she was not the kind to give in, so in a little while she began to arrange the duties among her small group of workers. But try as she would, her insufficient but willing staff could not quite cover even the absolutely necessary work.

I listened and wanted to help, but as I had no training at all, had never even been with sick people and had practically never seen blood, I did not feel very competent. Still, I was only too willing to do what I could, and offered to run errands, or "hand things," or obey any orders I from anyone. Madame Grouitch looked at me critically.

"Where we really must have help is in the operating room," was her tentative suggestion. "Someone must be there to wait on the surgeon."

The thought made mc feel rather queer, but I said, "Let me try." She did.

The first case vas a pretty bad one, but I made up my mind to do the best I could, and I got through without much trouble.

But the next case proved too much for me. We had a man whose head had been broken by a piece of shell and he was, in consequence, completely paralysed. There was some growth on his back, just by the shoulder, which had to be removed and I had to hold him in my arms to keep him in the proper position during the operation.

We had no anaesthetics. There was no money with which to bay them. The poor fellow was in a fearful state of nerves as he lay in my arms, screaming, but unable to move a muscle.

The feeling of his bare body on my bare arms, his screams, his breath, the odour of blood and the sound of the knife softly passing through the flesh were at last too much for me. I managed to stand it until the operation was over and then I went into the open air and was deathly sick. Five minutes later I apologised to Dr. Shuler and said I would be braver next time; and though it was a struggle sometimes, I was able to go on from that time without further mishap.

At the end of two days I was allowed to dress amputations. I would take off the dressings. Dr. Shuler would look over from his patient on the table and say, "Swab that with number two." I'd do it. Then I would rebandage the stump. The soldier would murmur, "*Fala, sestro,*" (thanks, sister) and hobble off on his crude crutches. Sometimes the tortured nerves of the patient would be too much for him, and he would lay his poor head on my arm and plead, "*Polako, sestro,*" (gently, sister) white great beads of sweat would stand out on his forehead. But usually they were so brave that it makes me proud to think that I was allowed to do what I could to help them. No one who has worked with the Serbian soldiers has anything but the warmest praise for them. The; are patient, gentle, proud and brave.

There was in that hospital many a boy of twenty with a gangrened wound for each year of his life. They would lie on their stretchers outside the door of the operating room, awaiting their turn, with their great eyes clouded with pain and misery. They would go upon that rude plank operating table with their thin bands clenched to help them bear the ordeal. We would put a lighted cigarette into their mouths and they would undergo the awful probing and draining of their sickening wounds without one murmur or moan—though I sometimes would put my hand over their eyes because I could not bear the look of agony in them.

The courage and marvellous endurance of the Serbian soldier is a memory that will often, I believe, uphold me and many, many others who have worked among them, when things seem too hard to bear.

Madame Grouitch was wonderful during these days. Not over strong herself, she was never too tired to soothe and comfort a feverish or suffering man. One day, just as she had declared she could not hold up her head another minute, someone came in from the street and asked if she could manage to give a very sick man a bed in which to die. He was brought in—a piteous sight, ragged, filthy, his beard and moustache matted together over his mouth and his dark skin gray with a deathly pallor.

"Then there is no hope for him?" asked Madame Grouitch.

"He cannot have eaten or drunk for days and there is not one chance in a hundred," was the reply.

"We shall see," she said, and took scissors and ripped away the ragged garments, the matted hair was cut from his face and with warm water she bathed the wasted body, then sat down beside him to fight with death. From time to time she forced drops of beef tea or brandy through the blue lips and hour after hour she sat waving a fan over his face to stir the sultry air and drive away the swarming flies. Her own fatigue forgotten, she waited, and many hours later had the joy of knowing that the man would live.

On returning to my hotel one day, after finishing my duties at the hospital, I noticed a small group of people standing about a shop window. I stopped to see what was exhibited, and found that it was not the window that was attracting attention but a broad shouldered young man who stood before it.

He was obviously a soldier. But when I got a full view of him I realised afresh that war, indeed, is hell. He had been captured by the Bulgarians during a fight on the Eastern front and afterward had been liberated and sent back to his regiment with hands bound. His ears, nose, lips and eyelids had been cut off. He had been scalped in such a manner that only a strip of hair, running from the middle of his head to the nape of his neck, in parody of a parting, remained.

Sick and trembling, I turned into the door of the hotel and the impression I had received made it impossible for me to sleep with any degree of comfort for many nights to come.

In talking with a Serbian officer some days later I happened to speak of this case and found that he was thoroughly familiar with it. Indeed he showed me a photograph of the young man, a handsome fellow, taken for his sweetheart before he left for the front.

It is not my intention to fill these pages with such horrible stories, but there were dozens and dozens of such cases as those described that came under my personal observation during my work in the hospital. Bulgaria was certainly a fitting Ally for the Hun to select in this World's War.

You must remember that up to this time I had lived a calm and peaceful life, such as most American women live. Horrors, bloodshed, atrocities had never before entered my life or my mind. I question whether I could even have read of them in the papers, and, if I had done so, I should have hesitated to believe that such things were possible.

But here, in war torn Serbia, my education in the grimness of war began.

On my return to England, where I was then living, after my work in Belgrade was completed, I felt that I was a different woman. Above all, there had come over me a feeling of the highest regard for that brave little nation, Serbia, and its gallant and heroic people.

CHAPTER 3

A Glance at the Country of Our Game Little Ally

Belgrade, the capital, before the war was full of curious contrasts: handsome, modern buildings and the rudely cobbled streets; peasants in gayly embroidered clothing and ladies in Parisian frocks; smart officers on beautiful horses and farm cart drawn by great creamy oxen.

The town stands high above the junction of the Danube and Save Rivers, and from Semlin, the Austrian frontier town, it looks like a hanging garden. After the flat plains of the approach to Hungary, the thick trees crowning the old fortifications are most grateful to the eye, and the gray walls of the prison-like fortress, with the white towers of the city, make an unforgettable picture.

On the principal streets are many fine shops, banks and business houses. The Konak or Royal Palace is a beautiful cream-colored building, set among trees and grassy terraces, while in the side streets are handsome residences, side by side with white cottage-like buildings, rather dark and ill-ventilated, in which the large families of the less progressive people live.

The sons and daughters of the well-to-do Serbs are usually given the advantage of a year or two of study in Vienna or Paris, and are particularly adept in learning foreign languages. The well educated Serb speaks German, of course, since the country adjoins Austria, and generally Russian, which the Serbian tongue strongly resembles. To these he adds French, and often English. Even the peasant, given the opportunity to educate himself, will frequently become a lawyer, doctor, scientist or writer, and it is little exaggeration to say that all Serbs are poets.

They are very proud and independent, and in spite of the fact that they live under a monarchy, they are the most democratic people I know. The Constitution of Serbia proclaims that "the king is to reign by the will of the people." In other words, if he displeases the people they may choose another in his stead. His eldest son does not of necessity reign after him.

By the Constitution of Serbia every man was entitled to five acres of land, two draught oxen, a certain number of pigs, fowls and some household furnishings, and these are his by inalienable right and cannot be taken from him even for debt. On this land and with these goods he must raise everything that he and his family eat, drink, use or wear.

There is very little money in circulation in the country districts, and when the family needs a cooking pot or other utensil it is acquired at the weekly market in the town by the barter of a fowl, some eggs, or a flitch of home-cured bacon. The women spin and weave the flax and wool, and make the beautiful, simple clothing worn by the family. They embroider these garments with silk and worsted, and many of them are real works of art and are handed down from one generation to another.

Serbia is now entirely an agricultural country, eighty per cent of the population living on and by their farms. Prizes are given to the farmers by a well organised agricultural society and the payment of taxes is usually made in produce. Every farmer gives annually a few days' labour to the State.

The farmers have all the sturdy qualities and virtues which come from close contact with Mother Earth. They are frugal, intelligent and industrious; all have poetry in their very souls. They are a peaceable, domestic people, devoted to their children and their homes, but they do not hesitate a moment to fight when those homes are threatened.

An odd custom has survived from the long Turkish occupation. When a peasant is obliged to introduce his wife to a foreigner he does it after this fashion: "This, may your honour forgive me, is my wife." But this attitude toward her is only for the outside world, for their family life is full of affection.

The peasant house is a low, white-walled, red-tiled structure with its windows and doors on one side. These being the only inlets for light and air, the houses are usually dark and stuffy, but each house is whitewashed inside and out frequently.

The Serbian family often pools its resources and forms a sort of community dwelling, called a "Zadruga." This consists of a large central house in which the heads of the family and the unmarried members live. Surrounding this are smaller cottages, called "*Vayat*," in which the married sons and their families live. The ruling member, or "*Stareshina*," of the house apportions the work each day and settles all disputes. Thus, if there were few very wealthy families in Serbia, before the invasion, there was no utter want and no beggars.

The country is very beautiful, with rolling hills and fertile valleys, and in no place in the world have I seen such a profusion of wild flowers; while the cloud-flecked sky which is characteristic of Serbia, the fleeting shadows over the glowing meadows, the broad plains with their golden crops and the myriads of bending fruit trees, make up a picture that can never be forgotten.

The climate resembles that of New England, even to the "Indian Summer," with its bright warm days and keen nipping nights. There are frequent heavy rains and thunder-storms during the summer months. The rough Serbian roads are full of deep holes into which, as almost the only attempt at repair, large boulders are thrown with touching confidence that the next storm will settle them into place.

All the hauling is done by big oxen, or by uncouth-looking water buffalo, who draw the crude carts at the rate of about a mile an hour. While it is a pretty sight to see these oxen decked with wild flowers by their peasant owners, yet it isn't so pleasant to find them lying by the roadside suffering from sunstroke, to which they are curiously liable.

Of late years the principal industries have been the canning of vegetables, the raising of pork, and the drying of prunes, of which Serbia has put forth a great proportion of the world's supply. Austria, desiring to swell her own commerce by the control of the Serbian market, has been able to deny this country an outlet to the sea. This has naturally hampered the progress of industries and Serbia has, therefore, remained poor—but not humble.

I have seen much of misery and want in that sad country during these last two years, but never have I heard a Serb, man, woman or child, beg,

They have always worked hard and lived poorly, but they were utterly content, since what they had was their own and their feeling of proud independence outweighed hunger and cold and even death itself. The peasant will bow before you and perhaps even kiss your hand, but then he will stand upright and talk as easily and freely as if to his own brother.

The hills of Serbia are full of iron, silver, gold and copper. In fact, in old Roman times the world's greatest supply of silver came from

Serbia, and her copper mines are perhaps the richest in the world. But jealous neighbours and lack of seaports have kept her from developing these rich resources.

Today, (1918), Serbia is absolutely devastated, as the Germans and Austrians cut down every fruit tree when they entered the country. It will take years and years of unremitting toil to give back to the world the supply of those delicious fruits and vegetables which the Serbian people formerly raised. This war will not be over when peace is declared. Years of reconstruction, of planting and patient upbuilding of ruined farms must intervene before Serbia is restored.

The Serb prides himself on his simple origin. King Peter says he is "of the people," and by his nobility during these years of woe and suffering he has proved himself a brother indeed.

The people were once light-hearted and merry, loving to sing and dance after the day's work was done, and, though for five hundred years the country lay under the heel of the Turk and the people were denied education, the splendid spirit of patriotism has been kept alive by song and story. Dearer than wife or mother is Serbia to the Serb, though he is a good husband and a tender son. To him his beloved country comes first.

The religion of Serbia is that form known as Greek Orthodox, but the peasant is naive in his belief that "*God helps those who help themselves.*" He is fond of telling the story of the man who fell into the river and called upon God to save him. So the Creator looked from Heaven and said, "Yes, of course, I will save you, but do move your arms and legs a little and try to swim out."

The men are splendid, handsome fellows, and even among the old men of eighty and ninety are some of the finest specimens I ever have seen. The women, owing no doubt to the lack of light and ventilation in their houses, are rather sallow.

The typical Serbian has dark hair and gray eyes, rather high cheekbones and strongly marked features; he has a tall and wiry body and is capable of withstanding extraordinary hardships. Always the battlefield of Europe, always holding the gate between East and West, and always loyal to her ideals, not even the Turk in his five hundred years of oppression could crush the religion or taint the blood of Serbia.

Serbia, like Switzerland, is entirely cut off from the sea, bounded as it is on the north by Austria, on the east by Bulgaria, on the south by Greece, and on the west by Albania. It was settled in the seventh century by wandering shepherd tribes of Serbs and Croats, who entered the western half of the Balkan Peninsula and there made their home. At the end of the eleventh century they had already formed a powerful State and were engaged in acquiring the culture of Byzantium and Rome.

Their greatest king, Stephen Dushan, was soldier, law-giver, builder of churches and patron of art and literature. In 1354, Dushan gave to the people the *Zakonik*, or Code of Law, which ranks high among medieval codes. Jugo-Slav literature, rich and glowing with tales of heroism, was born toward the end of the ninth century, and the earliest fragments preserved date from the tenth century.

The first Serbian novel, *Vladimir and Kossara*, was published in the thirteenth century. Among the first poetic writers were Marko, Maroulitch and Hannibal Luchitch (fourteenth and fifteenth centuries).

Serbia has always had the gift of song and sometimes her ballads are sung to the accompaniment of the *gusle*, an instrument shaped somewhat like a guitar but having only one string. It is rested on the knee and played with a high arched bow, and it is surprising what wailing, minor melodies can be drawn from it.

The Serbian language is very beautiful and lends itself admirably to splendid songs of valour, glory and hope. There is no part-singing, but all sing in unison. Sometimes two will start a song story in duet and when they cease two more will take up the theme and go on from that point, and so on until the story is done.

Owing to the depression caused by the continual wars for several years I had not heard the Serbians sing until in the autumn of 1916 before the recapture of Monastir by Allied armies—I found myself in a camp just behind the Serbian lines. It was a glorious moonlight night and the soldiers were filled with joy that they were again in their beloved land, so, after the frugal supper, a group of young men began to sing the songs of their country. The guns were booming near at hand and we could hear the rattling crackle of the machine guns, but through it all came the triumphant refrain of "*Givela Serbia.*"

In earlier days, when, for Serbians, education was difficult and culture rare, we find the burning names of Czar Lazar and his empress, Militza, educators and protectors of their people; Stephen Dushan, patriot and law-giver; Marko Kralyvitch, soldier and champion of the weak and lowly. Then after a long, dark time, during which the people were so oppressed that few names emerge from the murk, we see the Serbian brilliancy still undimmed, shining forth in the name of Vuk Stephanovitch Karagich.

Still nearer our time the names best known to us here in America are those of Father Nicholas Velimirovitch, the monk; the great portrait painter, Paul Yovanovitch; sculptor of historic figures, George Yovanovitch, and most marvellous sculptor, second to none in his genius, Mestrovitch. Also there are Rista Voucanovitch, native of Hertzegovina, and Murat from Dalmatia, but both Serbs and, before the present war, exhibitors in Belgrade.

We must not forget Stoyan Novacovitch, who was leader of the Conservative party. Prime Minister and Diplomat, nor Dr. Voya Velikovitch, prominent in the Liberal party and a well-known member of Parliament. In medicine there are Subotich, Wutschetitch, Roman Sondermayer, Among the later poets the names of Rakitch, the writer of epic verse, and Jean Douchitch, called the "Byron of Serbia," stand forth conspicuously.

America owes a debt to Serbia for the genius of that famous scientist, Michael Idvorski Pupin, American citizen but of Serbian blood and devoted Serbophil, who holds a chair in Columbia University and through whose efforts many influential Americans have been aroused to a warm interest in Serbia.

Less well-known in this country, perhaps, are the names of Prime Minister Pashitch, the splendid statesman; George Simitch, for many years a leading diplomat; Chedomille Myatovitch and Dr. Vladan Georgevitch, statesmen and writers; as well as Milenko Vesnitch, who was the head of the Serbian War Mission that visited this country a short time ago, and Professor Sima Losanitch, who accompanied him, together with General Rashitch, all men who shed honour on the name of their country. Kornel Stankovitch, musician, and Marianovitch an author, famous at least in his native land, and Illarion Ruvarats, the historian. All of these later men of genius look back to their forerunner, St. Sava, who in the fourteenth century devoted his life to spreading education and a love of art among his countrymen. The greatest hero in Serbian history, Marko Kralyvitch, called "Marko, the King's Son," was said to be the offspring of a "Dragon" and a Vila, or mountain fairy. "Dragon" in Serbian poetry is used to designate a fearless soldier and constantly recurs in tales of warriors and great men.

There have been many legends written of Marko, who is popularly supposed never to have died but to sleep in a cave near the castle of Prilip. He is said to awaken at intervals and come forth to see if his sword, which he had thrust to its hilt in the rock, has fallen out. When this shall occur he will return to restore the empire which was destroyed at Kosovo in 1389.

The Serbian ideals are high and spiritual. For example, when there was a dispute between Marko's father and his uncle and "*Probatim*," (adopted brother) as to which should inherit the throne and Marko was called upon to decide the question, Jevrossima, his mother, counselled him. The mother's wisdom has been preserved in a national folk poem:

Greatly as Marko himself loved justice
Greatly his mother thereto advise him;
'Marko, thou only son of thy mother
Let not my milk in thee be accursed,
Do not utter an unjust judgment.
Speak not in favour of father of kinsman
But speak for the justice of the God of Truth,
It were better to lose thy life
Than to lose thy soul by sinning.'

The world heard an echo of these words three years ago when, in reply to the proposals of Austria that Serbia should make a separate peace, deserting her allies, and so to save her population from terrible suffering, Mr. Pashitch, the great Serbian Prime Minister, said: "*It is better to die in beauty than to live in shame.*"

Many of the Serbian proverbs are closely akin to our own and all show a deep appreciation of honesty and often a keen sense of humour. A few of the best known are as follows:

It is better to know how to behave than to have gold.
Woe to the legs under a foolish head.
Keep white money for black days.
It is easier to earn than to keep.
Without health is no wealth.
A cheerful heart spins the flax.
A kind word opens the iron door.
An earnest work is never lost.
Who does good will receive better.
Debt is a bad companion.
What is taken unjustly or by force is accursed.
As the master is so are the servants.
Mend the hole while it is small.
Who judges hastily will repent quickly.
He who works has much; he who saves has more.
If you would know a man place him in authority.

It is better to suffer injustice than to commit it.
Boast to a stranger; complain only to a friend.
The lie has short legs.
He who mixes with refuse will be devoured by swine.
God sometimes shuts one door to open a hundred others.
God does not settle his accounts with men every Saturday but in his
own good time.
The devil never sleeps.
More men die of eating and drinking than of hunger and thirst.
The Home does not stand upon the soil but on the wife.
Better a body in rags and a soul in silk than a soul in rags and a body
in silk.
Do not ask how a man crosses himself but whose the blood that warms
his heart and whose the milk that nourished him.
Victory is not won by shining arms but by brave hearts.

The heroic sentiments of men and women alike inflame the imagination and give an insight into the character of the people as nothing else can do. General Stephanovitch said to his soldiers when, on an occasion, they were depressed and seemed spiritless, "Brothers, it is to your valour and achievements that I owe my honours. Unless you are again worthy of your past, I will tear these epaulettes from my shoulders and fling them at your feet."

A Dalmatian Slav said to R. W. Seton Watson, "We have regained our belief in the future of our race."

A foreign doctor told him, in one of the hospitals, "If you hear a man complaining be certain that man is not a Serb."

A Serbian lady said to one who would condole with her, "I gave my son to Serbia and now my prayers dwell with me in his stead."

When Serbian soldiers were commended on some splendid feat in this war, they remarked simply, "With Marko Kralyvitch to help us it was easy enough." They believed that they had seen that hero of old days riding on his gray charger before them.

The Maiden of Kosovo weeping over her dead on the fatal Field of Blackbirds cried, "Ah me! I that am so wretched that were I to touch the green oak tree my grief would straightway wither all its freshness."

Said the victims of a former invasion, "Grass never grows where the hoofs of Turkish horses pass."

Volko the Outlaw was a true Socialist when he declared, "If I pos-

GENERAL MICHAEL RASHITCH, LEADER OF SERBIAN
ARMY IN RETREAT OVER ALBANIAN MOUNTAINS

sess anything any man may share it with me; but if I have nothing then woe to the man who will not share with me what he has."

When the Austrian *Landsturm*, elderly men, were called to the colours, some waggish Slav hung this notice on a tomb in the cemetery at Spalato. "Arise ye dead, ye, too, must fight for Francis Joseph."

A Serbian divine, preaching in Serbia's darkest hour, uttered these solemn words, "The land of Serbia is an altar and your brother's blood is the sacrifice." And of the Serbs who had fallen in the defence of their country a native poet wrote: "From their blood shall flowers spring For some far off generation."

The spirit of the people is shown by the stories of how the old parents advised their children. A mother to whom an only son had returned asked him why he was there. "Why, I am on leave," replied the young man.

"But suppose there should be fighting while you are away," said the mother. "You must go back at once to your regiment where your duty lies."

A Serbian regiment holding a position sent several times to ask for reinforcements but none came and the regiment lost heavily. Finally a corporal was sent back to headquarters and his message ran, "There are seven of us left, sir. Shall we go on holding the position?"

An old man found in an attitude of utter despair was asked his trouble. "You would not understand," he said. "But I had three sons. One was killed in the Turkish war; one I lost in the Balkan war and my last son I buried today."

"But they fell upon the field of honour which should be a consolation to you," was the answer,

"I knew you would not understand," growled the old man. "That is not what troubles me: but they have left five little boys behind and it will be so long before they are old enough to fight for Serbia!"

There are endless stories showing the devotion of the people and many pathetic ones showing how even the women resign themselves to all loss if it is for their country's sake. In Macedonia I saw a woman, accompanied by two little children, who I had seen, surrounded by her large family, gathering the crops in the fields near Vrgntzc. In a moment of forgetfulness, I asked, "Where are the others?" Inclining her head toward the Albanian mountains, she said:

"They are over there—with God."

Serbia still lives in the hearts of her people

35

REFUGEES AT IBEN

CHAPTER 4

The Plot

Austria's attack upon Serbia in 1914 was most cleverly engineered, since the excuse was the murder of the Austrian Crown Prince Ferdinand by a Serb. But behind this we see the hand of Germany, who was plotting to gain control of the route to Egypt and India. Her idea of world domination began with the hoped-for Berlin-to-Bagdad Railway, and she went about entangling the other Central European Powers that they might work for her ends and pull her chestnuts out of the fire.

Austria wished only to bully little Serbia and did not desire to enter upon a World War, in which she might have clearly seen that Germany would take everything worth having. She wanted to continue her policy of repression and extortion against the Slavs and to succeed perhaps in annexing more Serbian provinces, as during the years since Serbia had thrown off the Turkish yoke, she had already taken the richest of Serbia's northern territory by force and by crafty statesmanship. Her bitterness against Serbia perhaps was augmented by a realisation of her own injustice and by the proud courage and resistance of the Serbian people.

Austria knew that Serbia would never yield to her dominance, so she plotted even in the blood of her own Royal House. The youth who murdered the Archduke Ferdinand was a Serb, but he was a Serb of Austria—one of those unhappy expatriates who had been brought up to hold allegiance to the enemy of his own country and in whose brain whirled confused and perverted ideals of loyalty and honour.

So by way of making all the world see that she was not to be trifled with and hoping that the world would believe that she was injured and justified, Austria prepared to invade Serbia. When she was thrown out of the country the first time her surprise was great. When a second time she found that the small but gallant nation, which she had expected to find an easy victim, was again too much for her, her fury knew no bounds. The spectacle of her army fleeing before a foe much less than half its size—fleeing in panic, throwing its equipment away and screaming for mercy when overtaken, was not an edifying sight.

But Austria tried hard to "save her face" and again deceive a world which was now beginning to understand her game. Drawing her mantle of dignity about her as best she might, she announced that "our punitive expedition against Serbia is now concluded," and a derisive world rocked with laughter.

It was Germany who, acting behind the scenes in 1914, pushed Austria again and again into the fray, and who, in 1915, when Serbia was nearly exhausted, egged on treacherous Bulgaria to strike for revenge against Serbia and to defy her parent Russia. It was Germany who bribed and coerced Turkey into joining the attack and it is German guile that has Austria, Bulgaria and Turkey fighting for their very lives today, (1918).

Germany's dream, (1918), is to rule the world, and these dishonoured accomplices may be very sure she does not intend that they should share her throne. They are to fight for her, smooth her way and be her humble vassals;—her slave-drivers, but not the princes of her House. A poor reward for treachery, outrage, child-murder, and all the horrors of blood and infamy in which these deluded countries have sunk themselves! A mean wage this, for which they have bartered their national souls!

What Germany has done on the west to Belgium—the infamy of her invasion, the stealing of maidenhood for shameful purposes of alien maternity, the looting, burning and enslaving—her partners have done in little Serbia on the East. And even more, for Germany has committed her crimes coldly and under the cloak of "military necessity," while Austria and Bulgaria, filled with hatred of the people whom the one had robbed and the other betrayed,—these two, I say, have run like ravening wolves through the fertile valleys and over the blue hills of heroic Serbia, and in their wake lies utter desolation.

When the accounting comes of murdered babes, outraged and mutilated women, young girls sold into shame in Turkish cities, massacred old men and crucified children, cities razed and riches stolen, orchards destroyed and fair lands devastated—when this accounting comes, God in His Heaven shall judge these criminals and His thunder-tones shall pronounce their doom.

CHAPTER 5

The Debacle

When Austria decided, late in 1915, that the time was ripe for her final attempt to crush Serbia, she massed her troops along the Danube and the Save Rivers, bringing up her heavy artillery and providing for the attack enormous stores of shells and munitions. Knowing how gallant and determined was their opponent, they made sure of having sufficient force with which finally to overwhelm her.

But they had no easy task. All the world now knows how Serbia met this attack, how bitterly she contested every rod of ground and how only by the terrific outnumbering of her devoted men and the immensely superior strength of her enemy's ordnance was she at last subdued—not conquered, for Serbia's Army still is fighting, (1918).

In October, Austria had prepared to cross the river at Belgrade by an irresistibly heavy bombardment, during which they fired fifty thousand shells into the town, their avowed object being to kill as many people as possible and thus create a reign of terror.

They also had laid a curtain of shell-fire on the roads leading from the town, and hundreds of poor fugitives were killed. Men and women, little children, wounded soldiers who were taken from hospital beds; the gently-nurtured wives and daughters of diplomats, bankers and college professors; shopkeepers, Austrian prisoners, servants and all the varied population of a great city fell victims to this merciless fire and lay in heaps upon that Road of Death.

The Serbian troops had not replied to this fire, hoping that by refraining the civil population might be spared, and later on, after most strenuously resisting the enemy's advance, had withdrawn from the town. But nothing availed to restrain the implacable enemy, and so he looted, burned and killed as his nature prompted him. Gallows were set up in the public places upon his entrance into the town and wholesale executions followed.

By the intervention of Americans, who had been doing hospital work in the city, these gallows were later removed to less conspicuous spots. The Americans protested to the Austrian military authorities and were able for a time to relieve the appalled and suffering people from the awful sight of their nearest and dearest hanging shamefully before their very windows.

In the attack at the frontier and on the town poison gas was used. And this new and diabolical weapon—new at least to the Serbians—was more fatal than all the other methods of warfare combined.

The open avowals of Austria, Germany and Bulgaria that they intend to exterminate the natives is one of the tragic phases of the situation in the Balkans. The wholesale hanging of prominent citizens, the turning of machine guns on innocent inhabitants, the exportation of thousands of young girls to Turkey, where they are sold into the *harems*, the young boys taken into enemy countries to be brought up in military schools, the removal of the scanty crops and the awful treatment of Serbian prisoners, are some of the terrible methods by which this extermination is being accomplished.

Yet a great shriek had gone up in Austria during the previous evacuation of Serbia by the Serbian army over the rumour that the Austrian prisoners were dying in thousands as they were driven through the mountains by the Serbian troops. Undoubtedly many did die, as did also thousands of Serbian soldiers; but so many, many thousands were freed afterwards, or interned in Italy, that it is probable the mortality was far less than might seem likely in the circumstances.

Also, and this is admitted by both Berlin and Vienna, after the typhus epidemic the Serbs offered to exchange all their prisoners but received no reply to their message. Therefore, the Austrians have no cause for complaint, nor can we believe that their protests were seriously made, as a very large proportion of these men were their own Slav subjects whom they themselves sacrificed, on occasion, lightly and remorselessly.

In the final successful invasion the Austrian troops were in every way inferior to the Germans who stiffened Austrian ranks, but the Serbs were outnumbered at least four to one, while each enemy division had double the number of guns that the Serbs possessed. The asphyxiating gases used by the enemy were of great advantage, but in spite of all this he had to fight for every foot of ground.

Even the Austrian and German newspapers paid tribute to the

desperate courage of the Serbian troops. The loss of Serbian officers alone—great numbers of whom were killed in holding positions which while hopeless yet would give the Serbian Army time to get further away and perhaps to consolidate some more valuable strategic points—and the heroism of the Serbians, men and officers alike, form an example for the world to wonder at and to follow if they can. During this terrible fighting the Serbs actually took over a thousand prisoners including many officers. Then the Bulgarians came in.

They attacked Serbia on October 11th, 1915, though their declaration of war was not handed to the Serbian Government until late in the day on October 12th.

Germany had gained a worthy ally!

This new blow meant that Serbia now had to defend about one hundred and sixty miles on the Save and Danube, one hundred miles on the Bosnian front and two hundred and eighty miles on the Bulgarian frontier. The enormous task did not dismay the Serbians, however, for they continued to fight heroically though they well knew that this time their enemies meant to finish the job of annihilation. Here indeed was a gallant Nation at Bay.

Serbia's only hope lay in the prompt arrival of Entente aid, which had been promised and was daily expected but which did not come. So at last, when nearly surrounded and threatened with total extinction at the hands of its merciless enemies, the gallant array withdrew to the trackless wilds of the Albanian mountains.

All the stores and munitions, the guns and motors, in fact everything that could not be carried on pack animals, had to be destroyed, while the remnants of that gallant army stood by filled with bitter grief and despair. Despairing they vanished from their beloved land, only love for which kept them from self-destruction They had too little hope in those black days, but it was their duty to Serbia to do what they could to survive so that, perchance, if the Entente did not again fail them they might by some miracle return to fight once more to restore to freedom the Serbia who must now lie for a time groaning under the cruel yoke of a ruthless oppressor.

CHAPTER 6

Hells on Earth

When the French and English retreated to the Marne, the resistless waves of German troops rolled after them and engulfed thousands of gallant hearts in their overwhelming flood. Mars rode upon the storm of horror and drank his fill of pain and blood.

When the Serbian Army retreated before the foe, four times its own strength, it went *backward* facing the enemy and fighting every step of the way. When the great arsenal of Kraguevatz fell, in November, 1915, the friends of Serbia wrung their hands and prayed that aid might reach her before it was too late.

The king, in the midst of his soldiers, said to them: "My children, you have taken an oath to me your king. From this I release you. From your oath to your country, I cannot release you, but If you win, or if you lose, I and my sons stay with you here."

Old and feeble, suffering with neuritis and other infirmities, riding on a jolting ox-cart over the atrocious roads and with despair in his heart but still true to his ideals and the high courage of his race, his was a fitting spirit to guide such an army as the Serbians had proved theirs to be. And the soldiers, tired, hungry, worn and yet not overcome answered him with a shout of "*Givela, Serbia.*" No shirking here. These were men who would be faithful unto death.

The Crown Prince Alexander, stricken and forced to undergo an operation at Skutari, would not seek safety until all arrangements had been made to carry the last poor refugee away to strange islands and foreign lands where he might await in safety the coming of a brighter day.

When the civil population of Serbia went forth from their homes, fleeing from those remembered horrors of invasion, they took with them only what they could carry on their backs, the clothing they wore and the bread which was to sustain them for a little—such a *little* time. Some oxcarts there were, to be sure, but these moved slowly and had to be abandoned for lack of roads when the mountains were reached. Here there were only rough tracks made by goats or mules and even these were soon lost under the pitiless snow. The animals were first turned loose and later, as the distress and hunger of the people grew more acute, they were struck down and their flesh eaten by the starving wanderers. Famished dogs went wild and made common cause with the wolves and bears which roamed the mountain slopes. Then woe to any poor soul who might become separated from his group.

The government formed all boys between the ages of seven and seventeen into companies so that youth might not be hampered by age in the flight. Over thirty thousand of these lads entered the snowy passes and what they braved, suffered and endured beggars imagination. Only six thousand survive today.

Had they fallen into the hands of the enemy various fates might have overtaken them. Any boy over twelve years of age was liable to be called a "soldier" and interned, then starved as all Serbian prisoners are starving today, (1918). Or he might be termed a spy and shot or infamously hanged as so many thousand Serbians have been within these past two years. Or, if still young enough to forget, he might be taken into strange lands and there trained in arms, eventually to fight against his own country.

So they went forth on their pilgrimage of martyrdom. Their doom has moved a warring world to futile tears.

Those awful roads in November were filled with a procession of women, children, old men and maimed soldiers striving to get away from the sound of guns—while behind them fought the little groups of devoted men, fought till their weapons fell from their hands, fought still when, wounded, they sank upon the blood-soaked soil of Beloved Serbia, fought to give time for those poor refugees to get a little farther away that perchance they might somewhere find safety.

Away in the icy roads leading to Albania, the poor ones struggled on. Mothers with their little ones around them; blinded soldiers led by the gentle hands of young girls, and carrying in their arms sick or half-frozen children; old men, tottering, stumbling, falling at last to rise no more; strong and handsome women, haggard now with bitter fear, their danger greater than any other.

A child would moan in its mother's arras, and its little life would

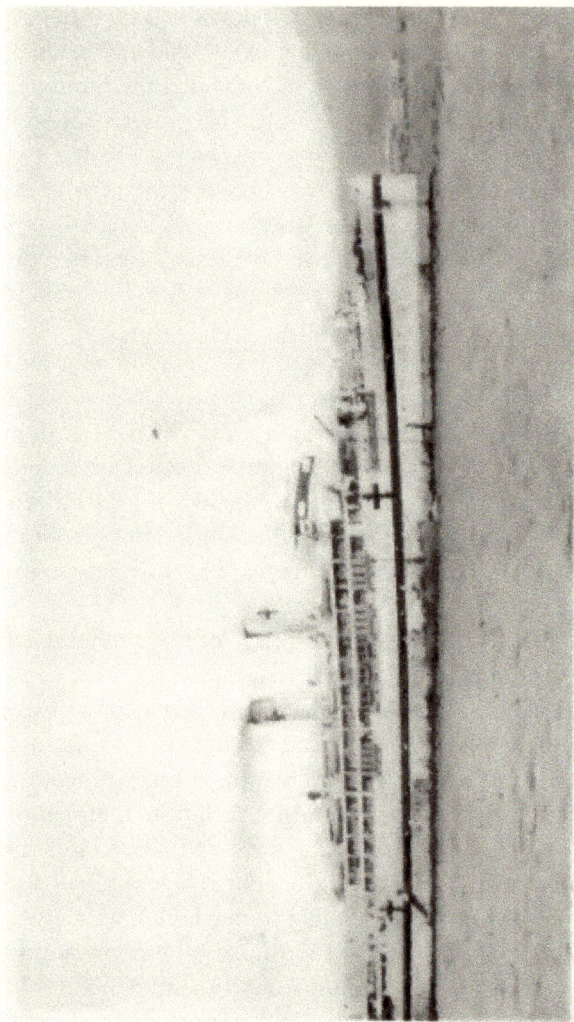

RED CROSS HOSPITAL SHIP "SPHINX"

flicker out. The mother, kneeling beside the tiny form, would take off her great homespun apron that she might leave the loved body decently covered. But the other suffering children, crying at her side, needed the meagre warmth of the ragged garment, so the heartbroken mother with a piteous prayer must gather her little brood about her and, leaving her baby uncovered, go on again.

One by one the children would fall by the roadside, prey to every cruel chance of misery, until at last the poor mother, more able to stand hardship than the little ones, would be left alone. Death would have been very sweet to her—to the thousands like her who made that awful journey,—but she was of mettle too stern to accept this compromise with Fate. She knew just three shining words, Love, Home, Duty. It was her duty to go on and keep life in her starved and freezing body as long as she could so that if, by some unimagined chance she might come back again; come Home and raise up other children to live in the Beautiful Serbia of her love.

Oh, these were soldiers too. Not theirs the reek and riot, the heat and joy of battle. They fought the bitter fight with cold and hunger. Their tired and bleeding feet trod the ways of Gethsemane; the rich and tenderly nurtured side by side with the poor and lowly.

Sometimes a terrible blizzard would sweep down upon them and they could not crouch down seeking shelter under the rocks by the rough trail but must needs struggle on since to falter then meant death by freezing.

Alas! for the many tiny hands and little feet which today bear terrible proof of the power of those icy blasts, and alas for the desolate mothers whose babes knew no other winding-sheet than the spotless snow and whose little bodies lie thickly on the road to a nation's Calvary.

On Corfu and Corsica, whither the Allies transferred the refugees when at last they arrived at the coast of Albania, so many died from the effects of that piteous evacuation that the islands; could not accommodate all the wasted bodies within their soil, and they had to be loaded on barges by hundreds, taken away from the shore and committed to the keeping of the sea;—that sea which in life had been denied them but which must now forever be hallowed to Serbia by the devoted hearts that have found rest beneath its waves.

Thousands of Serbian soldiers were taken prisoners in those terrible days of fighting. And what was their lot?

The treatment of prisoners in Austria—proud, aristocratic

English home of the author

Austria!—is awful beyond words. Forced to work at the hardest and vilest tasks, fed upon so-called "turnip soup," which is little more than unclean water, and foul scraps of unspeakable black bread—too little of either even to dull the edge of appetite, they are herded in draughty sheds without blankets and with only an occasional ragged sack to cover their wasted bodies. Sick and well are crowded together, without medical attention, and when a man grows too weak to work he is thrust into a wooden cage and there kept until merciful death lays its hand on him, and he can carry his sorrows into an unmarked grave. Beaten with the butts of rifles, savagely smashed into their faces, kicked, spat upon and cursed, these men still cling to life hoping they may yet, by some miracle, be freed to strike again for the Serbia of their dreams.

Looking backward and comparing the demeanour of the prisoners of different nationalities, the thing that impressed me most when I was in Serbia in 1915 was the air of utter and serene contentment on the faces of the Austrian prisoners; and in 1916, the suspicious, but relieved, air of the Bulgarians, when they found that they were still alive and unharmed after being taken by the Serbians.

The Austrians sang and joked at their work and, except for an occasional homesick boy, seemed to be thoroughly enjoying themselves. But the Bulgarians could not believe that their captors—who had seen the mutilated bodies of their brothers rescued from the enemies' bloody hands—would not take revenge upon them in kind. Serbian soldiers know only too well what it means to fall alive into the hands of the Bulgarians, for the Bulgarian is a Tartar with all the cruel instincts of the race. He kills his enemy as he lies wounded or shoots his prisoners in batches. Happy are these if death alone awaits them after capture.

In Belgrade I have seen pitiful remnants of men who have been rescued from the hands of the foe, whose favourite trick is to mutilate in some horrible manner that will either make those who look upon his victim shudder with horror, or rouse one to sorry laughter, as in the case of the wretched man of whom I spoke in a previous chapter. In either case the man is barbarously marked for life.

CHAPTER 7

The Call

From the time that I returned to England, where I was then living for a while, after the close of my hospital work in Belgrade, life had been smooth and pleasant. My home in lovely Hampshire seemed dearer than ever, with its great trees and its green lawns. The days slipped by so peacefully that the suffering I had seen seemed almost like a dream—yet not *quite* a dream, for always there was work to do, money to be raised, clothing to be collected and sent off to Serbia, letters from the friends I had made in Belgrade and replies to be sent. And always in my heart grew and flourished the love and admiration which had been implanted there by the courage of those splendid soldiers and by the patience and suffering of those brave and gentle women.

Early in 1915, a meeting was held in the Mansion House in London, by the Serbian Relief Fund, at which Herbert Samuel, T. P. O'Connor and other prominent speakers told of the terrible conditions in Serbia. The horrors of the typhus epidemic were so vividly presented that more than one person in the audience was moved to volunteer to go out and minister unto agonised Serbia.

I was one of those to offer my services. My former experience among the soldiers in the hospitals gave me reason to believe that I could again be of help, but on application to the Serbian Relief Fund I discovered that the fact that I was not "trained" and had no certificates rendered me unacceptable; my knowledge of the people, their customs and the practical experience I had gained among them, being apparently of little value. However, a week later. Princess Alexis Karageorgevitch, the American wife of Prince Alexis of Serbia, cousin of King Peter, wrote to me, saying:

I hear the Serbian Relief Fund would not take you, but if you will go out with us, Alexis and I will be only too glad to have you. We know how much every pair of willing hands is needed.

Then followed a hectic week of preparation. Vaccination, inoculation against typhoid, proper clothing in which to do any work that might be required of me, settling up all my affairs in case I did not return, and dozens of other things, including passports, all of which I had to attend to myself.

Prince and Princess Alexis had been collecting medical supplies and money for the stricken people. Mrs. Leggett, an American living in London, had given a splendid ambulance, and many committees in England and America had collected clothing, dressings and drugs, all of which were sent direct from England to Salonika, there to await our arrival.

Captain Nicholas Georgevitch was acting as *aide* to the prince, and it was splendid to see how he worked. He would trust no one to mark the many bales and cases containing the precious stores, and I was much impressed to find this immaculate young man kneeling on dusty warehouse floors with a stencil in one hand and a brush dripping with black paint in the other, solemnly putting on the addresses. I asked him why he did not have it done by the packers.

"If *these* things go astray, it is *my* fault!" was his answer.

We crossed from Folkestone to Boulogne and went through endless examinations though, owing to the high rank of the prince, I was told these formalities were less severe than ordinarily is the case. Prince Alexis having lived many years in Paris and being well known there, the authorities were very considerate on our arrival at the station, and we were able to set off with little delay for the hotel. The streets were filled with black-robed women and children and with blue-gray clad soldiers. On every face was a look of grave determination. I seemed to see written there those heroic words of the French commander: "THEY SHALL NOT PASS:"

I was hurrying one day along the Champs Elysées when I saw a sad little group of soldiers, real "*poilus*," brown and bearded but with the hospital pallor showing through the tan, wandering aimlessly under the trees. One was on crutches—his right leg missing; another had only one arm, while the third, with a green shade over his eyes, had his head swathed in bandages. They were evidently strangers in Paris, perhaps from the Northern invaded provinces, and certainly homesick and lonely.

As I looked, suddenly a gorgeous, glittering automobile came purring smoothly down the road driven by an immaculately-groomed man of middle-age—and this was an unusual sight, for few private cars were in use in Paris. With a gentle swerve the beautiful car drew up at the curb and the owner leaned out and said something to the three soldiers of which I caught only the words "*Mes freres*—" (my brothers).

The invalids stared in uncomprehending wonder, but the gentleman spoke again and waved his arm hospitably toward the *tonneau*. Slowly the soldiers smiled! Then they feebly lifted themselves, their sticks and crutches into the luxurious vehicle (with many injunctions to each other to be careful), and the last I saw of the party they were whirling gayly away amid the blessings and cheers of a little crowd which, like myself, had watched the pretty episode.

After dinner the first evening, Prince George of Serbia, eldest son of King Peter, came in and I was able to observe, without seeming to do so, this interesting personage. Very tall, almost gaunt, with broad shoulders held in a slightly stooping position and with hands always buried in his trouser pockets, he reminded me strongly of his father the king. Abrupt and restless, utterly careless of the conventions, said to be kind, but never tender, a passionate hater and an ardent patriot. Prince George has much of the charm of a high-spirited and undisciplined boy.

Surprised to see him in Paris at this time, someone asked, "And were you in this campaign, your Highness?" Instantly, his eyes blazing, he opened his tunic and shirt to expose his lean, brown body with a fresh and flaming scar. Then, turning, he showed a corresponding one at the back where the bullet has passed out.

"You think I do not love my country," he exclaimed. "Well, there's my proof."

Then I was told the story how, in the midst of a fierce battle, he had come upon a group of Serbian soldiers, dazed and idle.

"What are you doing?" he demanded.

"Prince, our officers are all killed and we do not know what to do."

"Follow me," roared George, and he dashed into the Austrians' front rank. The men did follow and when the enemy had been driven back they returned bringing the prince helpless and bleeding profusely but still full of fight.

After a few days in Paris, we started for Marseilles. Our party formed a fairly imposing spectacle. There were the Prince and Princess Alexis, Captain Georgevitch, myself, the princess' English maid, her French chef, the French chauffeur, (who was to keep the ambulance and the touring car in order, driving them whenever required) the chauffeur's wife, who was to be chambermaid, a pair of bulldogs, an Italian dog, delicate and beautiful, called Roma, and a tiny Pekinese. There were thirty-eight trunks, some of them filled with household linens, curtains and silver; for the prince and princess intended taking up their permanent residence in Serbia. How little we then thought of the further terrible events so soon to overwhelm the country.

Our first stop was at Malta, where we went ashore. The streets were hot and glaring with sunshine which was most cheering after the cold raw bleakness of London and even Paris. The governor sent a launch to take us on a trip in the harbour and we were much interested to see the battleships, destroyers and other vessels, and the enormous piles of shells and cases of various munitions lying on the quays ready for trans-shipping.

England was preparing for war at last on a large scale. Hospital ships were arriving from Salonika and even farther East, filled with sick or wounded, large numbers of whom came from Gallipoli. The streets of Malta were full of troops and staff officers, while convalescents, and soldiers returning from India on their way to the front, chatted at every corner.

A few days later we arrived at Athens, where we were met by Count Mercati, Court Chamberlain to Queen Sophia of Greece, and son-in-law of Princess Alexis. We had a delightful day and were sorry to leave when our ship sailed. The three little grandchildren of Princess Alexis saw us off with assurances that they would soon come to see us in Serbia,—"As soon as you have got everyone well," said eight-year-old Daria.

We had on board several French officers who were going to join their forces at Lemnos, two infantry officers in the beautiful blue-gray corduroy field uniform, an aviation hero, handsome and bashful as a girl but the holder of two of the highest French decorations for valour, and a dozen other interesting personalities, including an English officer on a mission for the Admiralty.

We touched at Dedeagatch, the Bulgarian port (then neutral) where all stores and supplies for the allied troops at the Dardanelles

OUTFITTING REFUGEE CHILDREN IN MACEDONIA WITH CLOTHING FROM AMERICA

were landed, and we could hear the thunder of the big guns as the warships waged their fruitless fight to pass the Narrows.

We watched the supply ships lying at anchor, with the sailors' washing whipping in the wind. We saw the bare, gray warehouses on the shore and pyramids of cases with pigmy figures of soldiers swarming over them, building them up or carrying them piecemeal away. Over all hung a heavy dim-coloured haze brought by the wind from beyond the sheltering hills. This was the smoke of battle! Over us the lowering clouds and below a sullen, choppy gray sea—fit setting for the tragedy that was soon to follow the Allies' expedition against Constantinople.

From Dedeagatch to Salonika is but a short journey, and I am happy to say we arrived during a brief interval of fine weather, so that my first view of the ancient Macedonian city was a highly satisfactory one. My previous two trips to Serbia had been made overland. The beautiful curving harbour encircled us, its shores jewelled with blue and pink and milk-white villas in an emerald setting of trees; before us the quays and modern houses of the town with the famous White Tower at one end and the small dark Custom House at the other. Climbing up the hill was the Old Town, with its quaint tumble-down houses and mosques with their delicate minarets, all surrounded by the wall which has been its protection for many centuries. Across the harbor sat Mount Olympus crowned with snow.

All the hotels are on the quay side, or near it. We went directly to the "Olympos Palace" and were so fortunate as to find excellent rooms. Our arrival caused some excitement. The prince and princess were overwhelmed by callers and deluged with invitations, most of which were evaded.

We found that our mountain of stores had arrived but the boxes were scattered and buried in the dilapidated, untidy storehouses on the quay. It seemed an almost hopeless task to reclaim them, but the prince and Captain Georgevitch, working day after day, with their own hands, dug through tons of freight and at last managed to get all our bales and cases together in one place. What their opinion of Greek porters was I dare not state!

This took ten days, but finally we started on the last lap of our journey over the plains of northern Macedonia where symmetrical little hills rose suddenly from the flat earth; past miles of swamps filled with rank weeds; sometimes, between clumps of tall marsh grass, catching a glimpse of lily-ponds where blue-gray herons dozed among the

MOUNTAINS OVER WHICH THE SERBIANS RETREATED

flowers, and occasionally meeting to our amazement a shepherd so primitive in dress and appearance that he seemed as though translated directly from the days when the gods dwelt on Olympus. Then, in the distance, blue hills and our train puffed slowly around a long bend and into Serbia.

CHAPTER 8

Through Beautiful Serbia

Ghevghelia is the frontier town of Serbia, and it was there we saw the first concrete signs of war. Just over the hills which here form the boundary between Serbia and Bulgaria a *comitadji* (brigand band) of two thousand Bulgarians was lying in wait to sweep down on the town—to loot and burn and destroy.

But near the station Serbia's guns were trained on these same hills and her tall gaunt soldiers were alert and ready to repel the invaders. Up the hillsides clung the tents and grass huts of the troops, while along the railway line low gray wooden crosses marked the graves of those already fallen in defence of their country.

The old men and young boys who were strong enough to carry guns, but who could not stand the rigors of campaigning, were everywhere guarding the railway lines. It sometimes hapened that roving bands of Bulgarians would creep down the hillside and surprise them. Then fresh graves and new crosses would appear along the line.

It was no uncommon sight to see boys of fourteen and men of eighty standing by the track, or sitting by their huts of cornstalks close by, and always with their guns held in their brown hands or coddled in the crook of their arms. Always ready, weak or old though they might be, yet were they strong enough to give the signal when danger threatened and, if need be, to lay down their lives for the country which they loved.

At this time Bulgaria was not *officially* at war with Serbia, but there is no doubt whatever that these bands of brigands were employed by Austria to harass the Serbians in the south and east, so as to keep as many soldiers as possible engaged there.

The last time that Austria's Army was driven out the retreating forces left an enormous number of sick and wounded behind them and among the sufferers were many with typhus. The infection quickly spread and soon the deaths were so numerous that in the smaller villages the dead could not be buried. The only way the bodies could be disposed of was by piling rubbish in the doorways of the houses where such deaths had occurred and setting fire to it. In this way the contents were burned, and with them the various vermin, which were the chief factors in spreading the disease, were destroyed.

From Ghevghelia, we travelled north, through Uskub where Claude and Alice Askew, English novelists (who had been doing splendid work in Serbia and who have since lost their lives on a torpedoed vessel) came to the station to greet the prince and princess and to bring the latest news of how the work was progressing. We learned of the death of many of the doctors, nurses and other relief workers who had gone out from England, France and America as soon as the typhus epidemic made its appearance. But in no case was any worker willing to leave Serbia. From the time the great need of help was made known, volunteers came in large numbers, fearless and ready.

There are graves in Serbia today of foreign men and women whose names are imperishably engraved on Serbian hearts. Among these martyrs to the cause of mercy were Madge Neil Fraser, Scotland's girl golf-champion, who died during the typhus epidemic, martyr to love and duty; Richard Chichester, heir to a great British title, worker and philanthropist; Mrs. Hadley, sister of General French, who was killed by a (bursting shell a few months ago in the presence of her daughter, while on duty at Monastir; the American Dr. Cooke, typhus victim, and Emily Louisa Simmonds, an American Red Cross nurse who offered her all and suffered much for Serbia. There wore many others also, heroes all, who gave their lives for a country not their own—who died nobly for the sake of a suffering people.

When we arrived at Nish, we found that the train for Vrgntze, our destination, had gone. The station master made up a "special" for us and we started out in pursuit of the "local." On overtaking it, we found it crowded with sick and wounded, who were being sent to the hospitals at Vrgntze, and with other workers like ourselves. Space was made for us however, and we went rattling away over the beautiful rolling valley of the Morava.

The single track railway wound in and out among the hills and through little towns and villages, whose white houses with glowing, red-tiled roofs were set in small gardens that later on would be gay with roses, lilies and pink oleanders. Sometimes we could see the larger house of a *Zadruga*, surrounded by its cultivated fields and by the smaller cottages clustering like white chickens around a mother hen. The trees of the fruit orchards sheltering the little homesteads would soon be bursting into leaf. In the muddy ditches ducks quacked and paddled, while long lines of solemn geese raised their heads inquiringly toward the passer-by.

Often in the towns, we would see the domes and minaret of a Moslim Mosque (rising side by side with the tower and Cross of the Orthodox Church), reminding us of the long Turkish reign. We happened to pass along the route from Nish to Vrgntze on a market day, so the roads were full of gayly clad peasants leading their small donkeys or driving the slow moving, dreamy oxen.

Sometimes a detachment of cavalry would dash from a gap in the hills and for a time gallop besides our not-too-swiftly-moving train, or a column of Austrian prisoners in their stained and ragged uniforms would pass, unarmed and almost unguarded, to their work of road-making or reconstruction. They did not look sullen or unhappy. I was told that many were Austrian Slavs who were only too glad not to fight against those whom they look upon as their own countrymen.

After some hours we saw through the pouring rain, which suddenly swept round the shoulder of a hill, the dense grove of trees that shelters beautiful Vrgntze, and in a few moments our locomotive puffed wearily into the station, which is two miles from the town. All the notables of the district were at the station to meet their Highnesses, and there was a long and rather damp reception.

We found the princess' automobile, which had preceded us from Salonika, waiting, and were soon on our way to town. The road was so bad we had grave fears for the springs, but we arrived without accident and were soon eating a good hot lunch in the Villa Agnes, which was to be our home. This villa was the only available house suitable for the food-sized establishment of Prince Alexis. The owner moved out shortly after our arrival and the whole place was turned over to him.

In spite of the rain, which continued to fall in torrents, I thought I had never seen a more beautiful place than Vrgntze. Imagine a little L shaped valley between blue hills thickly clad with trees and starred with white villas. Through the valley runs a tiny river only about ten feet wide but making enough noise for a stream three times its size. On either bank are gravelled walks which spread and wind away under great acacia and lime trees, and beyond the lovely park stand the villas of the townspeople, the shops, restaurants and *cafés*.

In the park near the river is a large open pavilion in which sometimes a band played. Nearby are the medicinal bath houses and mineral springs, for Vrgntze is a well known health resort, and the waters have all the virtues of those of Carlsbad or Ems.

But everywhere in the pretty town were evidences of the suffering that comes in war's train.

At the edge of the town is a large new hotel, the Therapia, which had been converted to a hospital by Professor Berry and his wife, Dr. Berry. Still further out, where the river spread in rippling shallows over a wide stony bed, was a long, low building—the Isolation Hospital. On the hillside above the town was a hospital run by an English Military Medical Officer, Major Banks, and near it a Convalescent Hospital under Mr. Gwin of California.

Many of the *cafés* and restaurants had been taken over and made into hospitals by the Serbians. In one I found Greek surgeons and a French matron, while among the nurses were Americans, English and Russians. The streets were full of convalescent officers and men, while the hospitals disclosed ghastly sights. Men lacking both legs and an arm, others with one leg and no arms, men whose heads had been broken by shrapnel or shell splinters lying paralysed, their tragic eyes following us as we passed. Young boys with minds unbalanced, sound of body but equally helpless, watched us stupidly, or shouted the mirthless laugh of sheer madness.

There was not room enough in the hospitals nor sufficient medical supplies for all the soldiers, so little or nothing could be done for the civil population.

Mrs. St. Clair Stobart, [1] a fine English woman, did establish roadside dispensaries where women and children could receive treatment. But, valuable as her work was, it was only a drop in the bucket of the awful need. Only for typhus could aid be given elsewhere, for of course it was imperative that this disease be utterly stamped out.

One day a woman staggered up to Major Banks' hospital and, falling on the doorstep, died. With her were two little children, both within a few hours of death. A corner of a crowded ward was cleared for them and I saw them just before the merciful end. In the same ward lay two strong men struggling for breath. They also died that day of pneumonia. Round them, the cots nearly touching so cramped was

1. *The Stobart Nurses,* a double edition, *My Diary in Serbia* by by Monica M. Stanley and *The Retreat from Serbia through Montenegro and Albania* by Olive M. Aldridge is also published by Leonaur.

ILYIA

the space, lay their comrades who wished to get well only that they might go out again and fight the implacable enemy.

On that day I went sadly back to my storeroom at the Villa Agnes and began unpacking a great wooden case which had come from America. In it I found several parcels of body belts, "cholera belts" we call them out there, and in the corner of each was sewn a tiny American flag. A sudden rush of tears blinded me and I pressed the little flag to my lips and broke down completely. The thought of my own countrywomen giving their time and devotion to help us do our work, so far away in that little known part of Europe filled me with appreciative emotion.

AUSTRO-SLAV PRISONERS AT GHEV GELYA

CHAPTER 9

At Work

When I offered myself for work in Serbia in the typhus epidemic, I thought I would be obliged to nurse the victims of that dread disease, but my orders were to take charge of the medical stores which we had brought and the further supplies which were to follow from various English and American sources.

My duties at Vrgntze began at 6:30 in the morning, when I was usually found in the storeroom opening up for the day. The round of the hospitals followed, and when I had secured lists of their needs, I returned to the store-room, unpacked and stored the contents of the large cases of supplies of various sorts which were arriving frequently from English and American sympathizers. Then I made duplicate lists of the requirements of each hospital, packed the goods on stretchers, which were brought up to the villa each day by the prisoner-orderlies, and received and filed the receipts from the matrons, or storekeepers of the hospitals.

Some of the hospitals, notably that of Professor Berry, had their own direct sources of supply, but the drugs, instruments, dressings and clothing which had been collected by the Prince and Princess Alexis did an infinite amount of good. By their great devotion and their thoughtful kindness to everyone around them, they endeared them-selves to us all. They were called by the soldiers "Our Prince" and "Our Princess," and no man was too ill or too sad to cheer, however feeble his voice, when the prince looked back from the door after hours of friendly conversation with the invalids and called out bravely, "Till tomorrow, comrades!"

The princess has a beautifully trained voice, and is a most accom-plished musician. There was a good piano in the Villa Agnes and each evening she would play and sing, to the comfort of us all after the often harrowing scenes of the day. Sometimes we would motor over to nearby towns on market-day, and come back with our car loaded with rude pottery, or native rugs and osier mats for the stone floors of the Villa.

About twice a week Princess Alexis would hale me forth from the store-room for a walk. We would go through the park and strike off into lanes where the fringy-petaled clematis made close fragrant curtains over the high, unkempt hedges on either side.

These rambles were a great treat after the strain of the sights in the hospitals and the hard, often manual, labour in the store-room. We would return with our arms filled with the gorgeous wild flowers for which Serbia is famous, and these would be massed in the great earthen jars by the doors of the Villa Agnes and in the little salon. With books, photographs and beautiful pieces of old brocade from the inexhaustible trunks, the bare, rectangular rooms took on a comforting look of Home.

The food was sparse and poor, but it was exquisitely cooked and daintily served. Now I happened to be possessed of robust health and a splendid appetite beyond what the others seemed to have, so these delicate meals did not satisfy me. However, I soon discovered a remedy.

Before leaving Salonika, I had been romantically attracted by a sign advertising "Honey of Hymettus." Shades of the ancient Olympians— it was irresistible! So when I started north I purchased a large wooden box (which got in everyone's way and was an absolute nuisance) containing four kilo jars of the famous honey. During the journey I often regretted my sentimental lapse, for I am not at all fond of sweets of any kind, but at Vrgntze that honey was truly a god-send.

So there might be no danger of my springing to the table and greedily devouring *all* the beautifully prepared but woefully skinny chicken which was to be "dinner" for four, *all* the small dish of salad, which had been painfully procured at great expense, and *all* the airy vanilla wafers which usually formed our dessert, I would retire to my own room before the meal was served and, locking the door, swallow three or four spoonfuls of rich, cloying honey and then take my place at the table with a politely dulled appetite. I never want to taste honey again!

As there was no plumbing in the Villa, all water had to be brought from the public fountains in big tins hung on a pole across the shoulders of a servant. Our water-carrier was an Austrian prisoner named

Basil. It was particularly difficult to converse with him because, curiously enough, his only language was Russian, and that of such a poor quality that even the Serbs could hardly understand him. For days he hung around the storeroom door and tried to tell me something.

From his contortions of face and body I was not quite sure whether he had a bad pain and wanted medicine or whether he desired me to get him a job as an acrobat. But at last I began to understand and to sympathise. He wished me to give him some clothes to replace the stained, old Austrian uniform he was wearing. When I had found him an outfit, he was the happiest man in Serbia, and the first time he appeared before the household we sat down on the door-step and laughed until we were weak.

Now Basil had a queer shape, broad and heavy, with short sturdy legs, long arms and a round, bullet head. His face, at the first glance, looked like that of a thorough-going ruffian with its squinting eyes, thick, blubber lips and flat, broken nose. But when he smiled, you saw that he was just a battered, kindly, simple soul with the heart of a faithful dog.

Imagine him then, in a pair of old dress trousers, heavily braided and six inches too long, a black calico shirt with large white stars and crescents printed on it, no collar but a big button at the neck of the shirt, evidently made of sealing wax, an excellent tweed shooting jacket with leather buttons and a belt which, not meeting, hung down his back below his knees. On his feet was a pair of glistening new "Arctics" and, coming down to his ears, which were forced out at an angle of 45 degrees, a flat-brimmed high-crowned derby hat of most ancient vintage.

As long as he was in uniform, Basil had saluted us in approved military fashion, but from the moment when he burst upon the family's astounded gaze in civilian clothing, his salutation consisted in depressing the brim or his great hat until it stood up straight in the air, then releasing it and letting it fall again upon his ears with a loud "*plop.*"

At our first view of the transformation the prince roared, the princess shrieked, the maids giggled hysterically; the chef, looking out of his kitchen window, chuckled until we thought he would have apoplexy. But Basil stood grinning with pride before us. Later, he beckoned me to the back gate with mysterious gestures and showed me a grayish bundle which he raised carefully in the air and then kicked violently into the road. As it fell apart in the ditch, I saw that it was his discarded Austrian uniform.

Another interesting member of the establishment was a Serbian *gendarme*, or soldier guard, named Ilyia, who had spent some time in the United States and spoke English quite well. He was a fine built fellow about six feet three inches tall, and broad in proportion and, though recently convalescent from a serious wound, was still quite the strongest man I have ever seen. He would take the big Red Cross cases, which two men could hardly move, from the ox-carts at the gate and carry them up the steep five hundred yards of garden-path with apparent ease.

He had made money in America and had opened a "*café*" in Pittsburg, where he was doing well, when the war began in the Balkans. His loyalty to Mother Serbia had brought him back to fight. One day. Prince Alexis asked him, "Ilyia, if you were so prosperous in the United States, why did you return to Serbia and leave it all?"

"Well, Highness," was his reply, "you see I felt I just had to kill some of Serbia's enemies—and I've done it."

When Ilyia was dressed in his dark blue uniform with its scarlet pipings, the white, blue and scarlet enamel "*Cocarde*" on his smart cap and high, well-fitting, patent leather boots, he was a handsome and an imposing figure.

CHAPTER 10

Austrian Prisoners

During the epidemic the Austrians, fearing infection, kept away from any possibility of contact with the Serbians. No fighting took place for many months and we were able to go about our work systematically without distraction.

The Austrian prisoners at Vrgntzc were a strong, healthy-looking lot of men, and though their uniforms were somewhat ragged and stained they were quite sufficient for comfort and decency. In the Park near the Springs was a stone and brick building which was used as a fumigating station, while farther away, near the Post Office was the prisoners' wash house where the steaming tubs were always full of linen, and even cloth garments.

The men moved about their work joking and whistling, seemingly well content to be busy and far from the battlefields. On the roads we would meet squads of them marching to or from their work, and the discipline was admirable as they swung along staring curiously at the princess who, with her golden hair and beautiful Paris gowns, naturally attracted attention. I may say here that, despite her dainty, fragile appearance, she did her full share of the hard and often distasteful work that demanded so many pairs of willing hands.

One day a group of prisoners stood at attention as we passed, and among them I recognised a waiter who had often served me in a London restaurant. They were always most respectful and never, I believe, gave any trouble to the authorities. The only cause for complaint I ever had against the prisoners was that when Arctics were requisitioned by the hospitals and I sent them on the stretchers with other stores, one or two pairs would always disappear *en route*. However, one could hardly blame the men, since footgear was so scarce that half the time their bare feet were on the ground. What with the sharp, coarse

QUAY AT SALONIKA

gravel of the paths this was no joke.

They were always most obliging and would move heavy cases for me, open boxes, or do anything else I might want done. Occasionally I would give them a few cigarettes, for which they seemed most grateful. The Serbian soldiers did not mingle with them, but I never heard any rough words addressed to them nor saw them treated otherwise than kindly.

In the hospitals, of course, sick or wounded prisoners were given the same consideration as the Serbs themselves. I saw one man lying at the inside end of the ward one day and apparently suffering greatly from the close heat of the place and a Serb, who was being carried in from the baths, had his carriers put him into that bed, giving up his own place by the window to the Austrian.

The prisoners lived in barracks at the edge of the town and were employed only for government work, but after Prince Alexis arrived one or two were allowed, as a reward for good conduct, to enter his personal service. This was very convenient, as few Serbs will take a menial position and servants are very difficult to get. The prince was lucky in finding a tall, handsome fellow, who had been an upper waiter in one of the best London hotels, and who made an excellent butler. With the chauffeur's wife and the lady's maid he did most of the house work, while the chef and Basil took care of the kitchen and the servants' quarters, which formed a separate building near the house.

The original dining room of the Villa was also an independent building, about sixty feet long by eighteen feet wide. This we used as our storeroom. Along one side I ranged packing cases, one on the other to the height of nine feet, and thus formed a series of very convenient cupboards in which I could keep the various kinds of stores, well sorted, and within easy reach. In an alcove at the end of the room, under a great window which opened on a terrace planted with fragrant standard roses, Prince Alexis had his desk, and here he and Captain Georgevitch worked faithfully day after day.

Among other things sent us from England, were thousands of pairs of knitted woollen wristlets that had been made for the Indian troops, who were transferred from the Western front to Egypt before these comforts were ready. As the Serbian soldiers needed socks more than wristlets, we ravelled them out and had the wool reknitted by Serbian ladies who volunteered for the work. We also had several thousand yards of flannel and a similar quantity of heavy cotton material which they made up into shirts. Even then we could not give the men a

PLACE LIBERTE, SALONIKA, (4 O'CLOCK ANY DAY!)

change of anything as there were not enough garments for all of them to be fully clad once.

In the centre of the long store-room was a row of stout tables for the workers, and all along the opposite side and down one end of the room were heaps of army blankets, cases of drugs, instruments, tinned milks, foods for invalids, and great, gray-painted chests of Red Cross supplies.

One day we received a large box with a black edged card tacked on it. Within were quantities of dainty baby clothes. These were soon sorted into sets and supplied to several poor, young mothers, widows of Serbian officers. These were the hardest of all to help, for they concealed their poverty so proudly that it took infinite tact to get them to accept anything at all.

Shortly after this Sir Thomas Lipton came to call on Prince Alexis. He was much impressed by our work and said that our store-room was the best organised and best arranged he had seen out there. I was much pleased, as he had seen them all, but, being an Irishman, it is probable the "Blarney" entered into his commendations.

In spite of the scarcity of many things—sugar being often unobtainable, and candles costing sometimes two *francs* each—we got on fairly comfortably, and came to realize how easily one can do without things that have heretofore been considered indispensable.

We all felt so remarkably well and strong that we began to look around for the probable cause. We thought we found it in the excellent water which was brought from the fountains and of which we drank large quantities, it being our only beverage. Wherever the Turk has been you will find fine wells since owing to his religion, which forbids wine or spirits, he will dig to any depth to gain an unfailing supply of pure water. For many who, like myself, will be unwilling in the future to patronise the German and Austrian "cure" places, I can strongly recommend Vrynyatchka Banya ("The Baths of Vrgntze").

CHAPTER 11

The Return

When the typhus epidemic was at its height very early in 1915, the proportion of deaths among those attacked was over eighty *per cent*. It seemed as if the whole population was dying.

When a stranger in a town fell ill his one desire was to return to his home, and no matter how far away he might be, he immediately set out on his journey. Of course he spread the infection right and left, so that the disease seemed to fly on wings among the simple and highly gregarious people. When we found out a method of segregating the awful malady in our district, the improvement was immediate and within a very short time the mortality was reduced from eighty to twenty *per cent*. Each suspected case was placed in a special receiving room, where he was shaved from head to foot, even the eyebrows being removed. He was then bathed with paraffin or some such insecticide and placed in an observation ward.

The vermin, which was the principal cause of the spread of the disease, now being eliminated, it was comparatively easy not only to cure the patient but to prevent any further spread of infection. Many nurses and doctors died before the invention of a special costume which rendered them immune. This consisted of a long tunic girdled closely; a pair of "Turkish" trousers bound tightly round the ankles; the head covered by a cap which completely concealed the neck; rubber gloves on the hands; the face and the insteps above the shoes were smeared with some ointment to repel the attacks of vermin. From the first week that these precautions were adopted, not a nurse or doctor who strictly observed them, was attacked. By dint of hard work, and rigorous attention to the many necessary details of sanitation, by mid-summer, 1915, the typhus epidemic had been practically stamped out.

Then we found that, for some unknown cause, our supplies were falling off in quantity, besides arriving with great irregularity, so I was sent back to England to see what could be done to insure a steady and unfailing flow.

As the train service was extremely poor, the prince offered to take me over to Stalac where I could get a fairly good train to Nish. The princess also decided to accompany me on this first stage of my journey and we started at four o'clock in a cool, gray dawn. The mist clung round the hill tops and a damp wind blew in our faces.

At Stalac we had a long wait, as the train was very late, but at last I was helped up the high steps of an incongruously luxurious railway car and, with kindly farewells, sent on my journey. As my command of the Serbian language extends only to a very limited number of words, Ilyia was sent with me to interpret and to look after me generally. I was to do many commissions, both in Nish and Salonika, for their Highnesses, and Ilyla was to be also my messenger and burden bearer.

At Nish I was met by a Professor Derocco, resident there, who had received a telegram from Prince Alexis to aid me as much as possible. By this time the rain was coming down in streams and we took a carriage, (which I am firmly convinced was the original One Hoss Shay), and started out to seek banks and consulates wherein my business lay. As I was to pass through Greece, Italy and France to England, it was necessary to have my passports *viséed* by the consuls representing those countries. The offices were full of people who also had important business to transact, and I had several long waits. However, as all things come to an end, at last I was free to seek food and rest, my mission accomplished.

Professor Derocco had found a place which he assured me I would prefer to the hotels, as these latter were all so uncomfortably crowded, and he took me to a large private house away from the centre of the town. We entered through a gate in a high stuccoed wall and found ourselves on a flagged path in a rain-drenched garden. Around the corner of the house we went up a short flight of steps and knocked at a glass panelled door. It instantly was opened by a quaint and charming old lady whose absolute replica hovered in the background. The large hall was lined with big wooden coffers and presses. Through the curtained doors of these furnishings I saw piles of the heavy hand-woven sheets and pillow cases, embroidered bed covers, and other linens that are the pride of a Serbian household. The shelves of another

RECENT VICTIMS OF GAS BOMBS DROPPED FROM ENEMY AEROPLANES ON MONASTIR

revealed row upon row of glass jars of fruit and syrups of which the people are very fond.

I was ushered into a pleasant room with great shuttered windows opening on the street. The walls of the room were ornamented with bright-hued native tapestries and the table cover was a brilliant specimen of hand-woven silk and linen threads finely embroidered. Coffee was brought in on a beautifully carved tray and that invariable adjunct to Serbian hospitality, a large carafe of sparkling cold water. I was told that this was the apartment used by Prince Paul, a nephew of the king, on his visits to Nish.

Professor Derocco left me to rest and went out to attend to some business for me, as the rain made it extremely disagreeable to get about the awful streets, and he was determined to save me all the effort possible.

At four o'clock he returned and, bidding my kind hostesses *adieu*, we drove over the yawning gaps in the rough cobble stones to the station. On the way I saw little groups of thin, ragged people crouching in the doorways, spattered by the pelting rain and by the mud from the wheels of our rickety, furiously-bounding cab. These, I was informed, were refugees from the North and East whose villages had been devastated by the Austrians and Bulgarians. Hungry, wet, uncomplaining, they sat there believing that soon all I would be well and they would be able to return, rebuild their homes and begin again to cultivate their little farms in peace and security. At the station we found a fairly dry table in the *café* on the platform and here we dined on cabbage soup, coarse brown bread, goat's cheese, dry prunes and beer.

Ilyia appeared when it was time to entrain. As Professor Derocco had arranged to pay a visit to his young daughter, who was living with his aunt at Uskub, he accompanied me. For hours in the train we talked of Serbia and her prospects. The professor, who is one of the government's cartographers, produced one of his maps and I learned far more of Serbian geography than I had ever known before. So engrossed in this study was I that if was after midnight before I remembered the full day I had had and my need of sleep.

My escort bade me goodnight and sent the porter to make my bed, and I was soon in a loglike slumber. This would have lasted, I feel sure, well into the next afternoon, had I not been suddenly roused by a loud and persistent rapping on the door. When I opened it there stood Professor Derocco, looking irritatingly fresh and immaculate, bidding me goodbye and begging me to let him know if he could serve me in

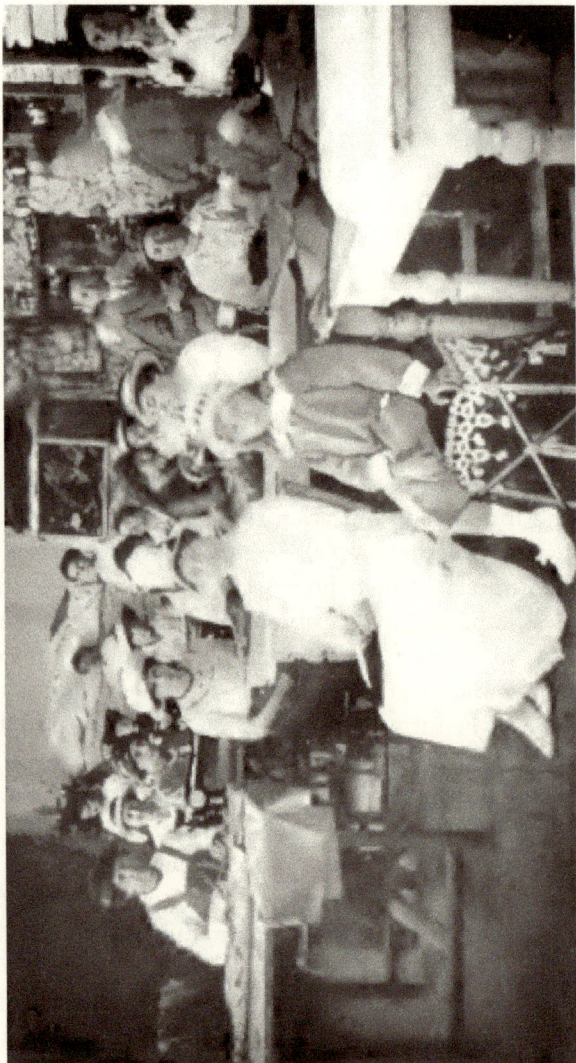

PRINCESS ALEXIS IN THE STORE-ROOM AT VRINTZE

any way either then or in the future. I did appreciate his kindness but, oh, how I regretted my interrupted sleep.

Arriving at Ghevghelia I was entertained by the officials who provided a light repast with a graceful and kindly hospitality that made it as acceptable as a banquet. Then again, the dull, swampy plains of Macedonia and, just as dusk began to deepen, Salonika.

A telegram had been sent to the Olympos Palace Hotel, but the courier who met me said that every room was taken and people were even sleeping in the reception rooms, while the writing-room had been turned into a dormitory for officers. However, he said he would take care of me or die in the attempt. So, with gigantic Ilyia on the box and the courier leaning out the door of the cab and shouting to clear the way, we rattled over the stones and around the corners until we pulled up before the Hôtel d'Amerique.

The old reception clerk showed me into a large room with three great four-post beds, all made up and with mosquito curtains snugly tucked in. I asked how much he wanted for it, and with an air of great surprise, he inquired if I meant "all of it." I said I certainly did, and he mumbled that the place was crowded and it would be very expensive. After a good deal of grumbling and sly calculation he assured me he could not let me have it under eight *francs!* I sent him for as much water as he could bring me—about four pails full—had a good refreshing wash and slept.

The next day was a busy one, and though my boat did not sail until midnight, there was none too much time. Ilyia was invaluable, and I kept him going from early morning until I bade him goodbye at the dock. When I tried to give him a gold piece for good luck he refused it, saying he was honoured in serving me since I was a friend of his country. I was deeply touched and we shook hands. I got to bed at twelve o'clock and stayed there until noon the next day.

CHAPTER 12

Doing My Bit in England and America

The journey to Naples was uneventful. There were some interesting people on board, mostly Italian Reservists returning to join their regiments. Among them was an "air-man," who had been training Bulgarian aviators (how he must regret it now). There was also an Italian editor from Constantinople and two Roman ladies, sisters, returning from Jerusalem. On this boat I made the acquaintance of Mr. Francis Markoe, who had been working with Lady Paget's unit in Serbia all through the typhus epidemic and who is now a member of the Serbian Relief Committee of America and still working faithfully for Serbia.

We went overland from Naples to Paris and when, passing along the Riviera, I saw men and women beautifully dressed, care-free, over-fed, I wondered which was the dream,—the suffering, hungry, ragged, courageous and devoted people I had just left, or this frivolous, perfumed, laughing crowd of pleasure seekers. The contrast was astounding.

On my arrival in London, I found the Serbian Relief Fund was packing and sending out large cases every week. Mrs. Carrington Wilde told me the organization was receiving splendid response to its appeals, and after I had seen the fine corps of volunteer workers packing and labelling the bales of clothing and the great boxes of other much needed supplies, I felt happier.

Soon after my return. Captain Georgevitch arrived with a collection of war trophies consisting of Austrian war rifles, knapsacks, shells, hand grenades, swords, drums and many other interesting trophies collected on Serbian battlefields. These he placed on exhibition in some of the large stores in London and in other towns as well. Winchester among them, where I was able to arrange for a show of them at the Guild Hall. We charged a small admission fee and afterwards auctioned off the things. The affair was a great success and we made a good sum to be sent back to Serbia in the form of drugs and other necessaries. In October, having finished my work in England, I wished to get my passports to return to Serbia, but the situation was by this time so grave, owing to the strong Austrian offensive before Belgrade, that the American Ambassador refused to let me go It was not long before we heard the terrible news of the steady advance of the enemy forces, the capture of Kraguevatz and then the retreat of the Serbian army—fighting every inch of the way—and the awful tragedy of the evacuation.

I thought of my many friends in Belgrade, of the invalids, the maimed and the old who had to be left behind, and my heart was torn with fear and sorrow over their inevitable doom. I knew that none but the very strongest could survive, that the weak and the ill would die of privation and that a deliberate policy of extermination would be carried on by the invaders. We know now that one-quarter of the population has already been destroyed and we fear that this is a too-conservative estimate.

Unless this war ends favourably for us, Serbia, will be but a memory and her brave and splendid people will die out, butchered by the crudest and most vindictive enemy the world has ever known. Serbia who held the gates on the East, as Belgium did on the West until the armies of England and France could take their stand; Serbia who, like Belgium, has been crucified and today, (1918), is gasping out her life under the tortures of *our* enemies!

After taking part in the dreadful retreat over the Albanian mountains, Princess Alexis wrote me imploring my help. She and the prince had started with their household in the automobile and the ambulance, she said, but on reaching the mountains had to abandon these vehicles.

The princess wrote:

We burned them so that they should not benefit the enemy.

She and her husband had passed through the awful ordeal, suffering from cold and hunger as did the poorest peasant in that fearful march, and those who saw her say she worthily upheld the reputation of our American women for courage and endurance.

After her arrival in Rome, she wrote a restrained and unsensational account of the horrible journey which was published in the New York papers. In it she nowhere speaks of her own personal miseries, but I have testimony of eye witnesses that she and Prince Alexis endured cheerfully with the others all the suffering and hardships.

After receiving her letter, I came home to America, knowing that if I could only tell the people of the terrible need of Serbia their generous hearts would prompt them to give. Nor was I mistaken. I myself joined the Serbian Relief Committee of America and undertook to deliver a series of lectures on Serbia. In that way I soon raised a substantial sum for relief work among the refugees on the Island of Corsica.

My object was to get as much help as possible to the destitute people, with the utmost speed, since every hour and every day counted tragically against them in suffering and death.

So as the Serbian Relief Committee of America had at that time no suitable organisation in the Balkans with which to administer relief to the refugees, I requested them to allow all funds which might be raised at joint meetings by Miss Burke, an Englishwoman who had now joined me, and myself to be turned over to the Scottish Womens' Hospitals (whose representative Miss Burke was). They had a relief station already established on Corsica and could give help without delay. As we cabled the amount in hand, the Scottish Women's Hospitals would draw upon their own funds pending the arrival of our money to replace the sums.

The most successful meeting held during the two months that we worked together took place at the Breakers at Palm Beach, and at this one meeting we raised enough money to establish a tent hospital of two hundred beds on Corsica which was to be known as "The American Unit of the Scottish Womens' Hospital."

This meeting was held under the patronage of some of the most prominent citizens from all over America, and our two most generous subscribers were Mrs. Alexander Hamilton Rice and A. Kingsley Macomber, Esq. In consequence of our arrangement with the Scottish Womens' Hospital, hundreds of lives were saved which otherwise would have been lost for lack of immediate aid.

Since then we have been able to send really good sums to carry on the work of feeding, clothing and restoring to health those destitute and unhappy people. The Serbian Relief Committee was so fortunate as to interest Dr. Edward Ryan of the American Red Cross in its work, and the last train loads of food sent into Serbia from Roumania by him were largely contributed to from our fund.

America was neutral then, the greatest and the richest country in the world. Her people provided with every comfort, every luxury. She was so fat and well fed it was difficult to realize that actual starvation stalked throughout so many unhappy cities in Europe. America did not realise that this war so intimately concerned her and that she would inevitably be drawn in. For a time there seemed to be something of the spirit which prompted the man of old to say, "*Am I my brother's keeper*," and to us, who had seen the trend of events, it was tragic that our country should be so blind.

Chapter 13

Through the War Zone

In August, 1916, we of the Serbian Relief Committee began to feel a touch of impatience in letters from our American Consuls at Athens and Salonika and, as personal business called me to England, I offered to extend my journey to the near East to see what could have happened.

We were now a world at war, and sea travel having become more and more dangerous, I had been warned that it was most difficult to get permission to cross, but owing to the good offices of Mr. Arthur Lee and Mr. John Barrett, both of Washington, I was soon supplied with a passport and with a letter from the Secretary of State, recommending me to the courtesies of the American Ambassadors, Ministers and Consuls in the allied and neutral countries through which I must pass.

It was the third week in August when I sailed. There were no trippers, no gamblers, no "little actresses" and few New York dressmakers or milliners on board. Everyone was going on serious business, mostly connected with the war, which was nearly the sole topic of conversation. Many people then, as they are today, (1918), were perfectly certain that—"Germany cannot last out another six months." There were several alarms of submarines and one man was so depressed by the sense of danger that he jumped overboard and was lost.

On our arrival at the mouth of the Mersey, we found ourselves enveloped in a dense fog and were obliged to wait several hours before we could go up to Liverpool. Just behind us, when we at last did berth, was a large ship filled with German prisoners that had arrived that day from the Cameroons. They lined the rail and stared at us curiously, and when two other New York women and I passed near them, one of the younger ones shouted something about "*Amerikanerin*" and spat viciously in our direction. I saw an English sailor grab him by the collar and there was trouble for a few minutes.

Arriving at the Carlton Hotel in London, I was informed that I must report as an "alien" at the nearest police station within twenty-four hours. So the next morning I went to Vine Street, and had a pleasant interview with a nice old police sergeant, who said I must let him know the day before I wished to leave London.

As soon as he had given me my papers, I began to inquire about permission to go to France. The French authorities were very strict about allowing civilians to enter the country and the English were nearly as obdurate about letting them out of England. But on appealing to Colonel Walker, at the Home Office, my way was made smooth by a letter from him to the officer in command at the French Consulate-General.

As there had been submarines in the English Channel lately, the boats often did not sail for several days together and when they did go, of course, they were very crowded. Armed with my passports, credentials, letters and a stack of photographs, I went to the Consulate very early in the day and obtained, with little delay, a French passport, which was warranted to get me into France but not to get me *out*. Then back to Vine Street to tell the Man in Blue of my intention to leave.

As a former employee of mine was lying wounded in a Red Cross hospital at Southampton, I applied for an "identity card" to enable me to visit him, but the old sergeant said, "Oh, you won't need that as you are to sail from Southampton. Just report at the police station when you get there and they won't 'urt you."

When I saw poor Mursell, my faithful gardener of happier days, on crutches and heard that he had been wounded in the legs, he seemed to think that I ought to have an explanation. As he is only five feet four inches in height he was, for a time, ineligible for military service, but after a while "Bantam Regiments" were formed and he was among the first to join and was the *tallest* man in his regiment!

"Yes, madam," he said, "I caught a shell splinter in my legs. Why a man *six* foot four could have been wounded there." He was quite cheerful and happy, in spite of the pain which he was suffering, to have "done his bit" in the great war.

On my way to dinner in the town, I remembered that my presence at the police station was required, so I went there. The sergeant on duty asked my business.

Bringing in sick civilians at Vrynatchka Banya

"I'm an alien and am here without an identity card," I said. "Are you going to arrest me?"

"What for, madam?" he asked,

"Oh, I just thought you might want to," I replied.

"Wouldn't think of such a thing. And I didn't know you was a h'alien, madam." This courteously.

I looked surprised and he laughed and said he remembered often having seen my husband drive with me down the High Street when we lived near Southampton and he 'ad h'always supposed that I was H'english though he knew that Mr. Farnam was a H'american.

At eleven o'clock the following night I went on board the crowded Channel steamer, but we did not leave the dock until six o'clock, broad daylight, and then simply *scooted* across. The crossing was really dangerous and every one of the several hundred passengers kept as sharp a lookout as if he were personally responsible for the safety of the ship. However, we landed at Le Havre unharmed, and after endless formalities were allowed to proceed to Paris. Such a long journey! We seemed to stop at every barn and cottage on the route and arrived at dead of night, as hungry and cross as if *our* troubles and discomforts were all important.

But just as we finished the short examination at the station gates, a train-load of wounded French soldiers came in and the first men were carried past us on their stretchers to the waiting ambulances. We stood ashamed of our peevishness when we saw the glowing eyes shining in the dim light and heard the feeble voices shout "*Vive la France.*"

The men about me took off their hats and the crossest, most cantankerous woman of us all, who had made the journey even more uncomfortable than need be by her constant grumbling, ran forward weeping and tried to kiss one pathetic lad whose blanket lay hideously flat where his legs should have been.

The streets of Paris were dark and the chauffeurs seemed to drive more recklessly than ever. I was glad to reach my hotel and find a cool, clean bed ready for me.

My first visit was to Dr. Milenko Vesnitch, Serbian Minister to France. We had an hour of discussion on the situation in Serbia and as to what was advisable for the Serbian Relief Committee of America to concentrate on in future. He said that the needs of the population still in Serbia were most piteous and urgent, also that we should form a fund to supply seeds and farming implements to help to restore the people when the war is over. He also suggested that America should

PRINCE GEORGE OF SERBIA, ADMIRAL TROUBRIDGE
AND THE AUTHOR

take up the hospital and medical work among the Serbian troops as this was sadly needed.

Dr. Vesnitch thought it unnecessary for me to go to Corfu as Miss Helen Losanitch was already on the spot and could report on conditions there and Corsica. But he said I should go to Salonika and talk with Serbs there to get a full idea of what was required. Also, he thought it advisable for me to go to Geneva and see M. Navelle who represents Serbian Relief there.

The French authorities were most kind and gave me the necessary papers to leave Paris without delay. At eight o'clock my train, packed with convalescent soldiers, who would never be able to fight again, on their way to their homes and many pale, emaciated civilians who were seeking health among the Swiss mountains, pulled out for the frontier.

In my compartment there was a young girl, clinging frantically to a tall handsome Serbian officer who, when the train was about to start, placed her, fainting, in my arms and begged me in a broken voice to take care of her. Later I learned that she had been a governess in a well-to-do family in Belgrade and had fled before the enemy, with her employers. The officer was her *fiancé* whom she had met again unexpectedly at Corfu, and who had been sent to Paris with important papers, and was thus able to take care of her on her long journey.

The poor girl was very ill as the result of the hardships she had undergone and passed from one fainting fit into another until I was nearly distracted. However, on reaching the Swiss border I found a party of English nurses who said they would take charge of her, as they were remaining there for some days and she was clearly not fit to go on. We sent a telegram to her father who, I heard afterward, came and took her home.

On my arrival in Geneva I went to the American Consulate for information as to what must be done before attempting to enter Italy. The consul-general told me that it would be necessary for me to see the Italian Minister in Berne, and it would be at least ten days before I would be allowed to go, *if at all*, since instructions regarding me must come from Rome. This was a blow.

As soon as M. Navelle's office was open, I went to him. He reported that Dr. Ryan, of the American Red Cross, who was, or lately had been, in Vienna, was hopeful over the condition of the country but we feared, on reading more recent statements of other observers, that possibly the doctor was unduly optimistic. Since then these fears have been tragically realised.

The reports as to the conditions of the Serbian prisoners in Austrian prison camps were heartrending and we agreed that aid to these starving men must be rushed at once by the Swiss Committee. As many of the English and French prisoners had so often said they could not have survived had it not been for the parcels of food sent them by their families and friends, we could well imagine the awful needs of these Serbian soldiers with no one to help them, their country being completely at the mercy of a cruel and vindictive enemy and their families destitute and living in abject misery. M. Navelle promised to send a full report at once to our American Committee so that no time should be lost and money and supplies might be forwarded to such an extent as our funds would allow.

At one o'clock the following morning, in a pouring rain storm, I left for Berne. I arrived at four-thirty and had a few hours' sleep before the Legations opened.

CHAPTER 14

Eastward Ho!

Our Minister to Switzerland, Mr. Stovall, was very kind but held out no hope that the Italian Minister would let me go into Italy until he had received advices from Rome. However, he gave me a note to the minister and I took a cab to the Legation. The driver stopped at an iron gate in a high wall and as I entered a great "police" dog came swiftly around the corner of the house but calmed down when I spoke to him. While we were making friends, the minister appeared in the garden and seemed surprised that the dog was so amiable as he was usually not at all friendly to strangers.

Then I was sent over the Chancellerie, which was next door, and was told to state my business to the secretary. By the time the minister came in, about ten minutes later, my passport had been examined and all my papers were in order. He shook hands and wished me good luck and I asked, "When may I hope to go, Your Excellency?"

"Why you can catch the 12:50 if you make haste," he said, smiling. I fled.

Back to the hotel—ordered my bill as I rushed to the elevator—grabbed my bags, paid my account on my way to a waiting cab, and hopped into the train three minutes before it pulled out!

At Iselle, on the Italian frontier, the examination of travellers was very strict and for some reason I was left to the last. When I went before the examiners, the chief, a dapper-looking young man, rose and bowed, asked me a few questions, waved my papers aside, stamped my passport "*Iselle*" and "*Entrata*" and handed it to me with another smile and bow; I thanked him thinking, "how kind everybody is," and started out.

But the man snapped "*Nella camerata*" and I was taken into a little room, stripped and searched. When I returned I found a group of men plunging their hands into my dressing bag and suitcase and turning the contents upside down. Every scrap of paper was scrutinised and discussed and every garment shaken out and held up before this crowd of men. The person who had examined me was the only other woman in the place.

A soldier found a pack of worn playing cards in one of the bags and told me these were forbidden. He said, "I must destroy them." I was so angry by this time, I could hardly contain myself but I said smiling, "Do what you like with them. Give them to your friends, or your children, if you wish." He turned very red and tore them in bits.

Into this heated scene strode the chief and demanded every paper I had with me. His questions were searching and peculiarly insulting while his manner was that of one who was dealing with a particularly vicious criminal. I handed over my credentials, my notes, card case, letters and even the newspaper I had been reading when I left the train. The latter he threw on the floor and in a very few minutes I saw that he had little or no knowledge of English. An elderly gentleman who seemed quite ashamed of the treatment given me, offered to read the various papers, which he did with some difficulty.

Then followed a long and very noisy argument. I gathered the first man had decided the minute he saw me that I was a spy, and his manner made me believe that my ultimate (Latin) destination would be the rock-hewn, undersea dungeons of some noisome Italian jail! His disappointment, when he found there could be no charge made against me, was a positive pleasure for me to witness.

My letters from the Secretary of State and from the American Ambassador in London (written for an earlier journey but equally good on this one) were too much for him. So at last I was allowed to go—after he had flung my papers down so that half of them fell on the floor and I had to pick them up.

Thinking it wise to show how dignified I could be under adverse circumstances, I sailed out with head high, smiling but with a hot, red spot on either cheek, only to be followed by a roar of laughter. On reaching my compartment I found that the desired effect had been rather dashed by a yard or two of pink ribbon from a forgotten bow that trailed behind me, and had in some way become entangled with a greasy paper bag so that my haughty progress must have resembled that of an indignant kite!

At Milan I found that the train for Rome had been gone an hour, so, lugging my bags which grew heavier and heavier, I went out into the rainy streets, discovered a small but comfortable hotel near the station, and had another all too-short night's rest.

At six-twenty, in a violent downpour, my train left for Rome and there I was lucky in catching the Naples Express. In the dining-car my seat happened to be opposite that of an Italian naval officer who glared at me ferociously all through dinner. When the coffee was served he could bear it no longer and pointing to the large enamelled Red Cross, which I always wore when travelling in the war zone, he demanded, "What is that you are wearing, *signora?*"

When I told him that it was the Royal Order of the Serbian Red Cross, he looked rather flat and said that seeing the two-headed eagle on it he could not think it anything but Hunnish.

At midnight the train crawled into Naples and my bed soon claimed me. In the morning I had developed such a cold that my voice had nearly gone. I asked when the next boat was to leave for Athens and the clerk said at noon that day, but I would have to apply for permission and then wait ten days for advices from Rome. I simply sighed "That's an old story," and sought the American Consul.

Mr. White, the consul, was most sympathetic but he did not know what he could do except to send his secretary with me to the *prefectura*, which he did. Mr. Garguilo first got my passport *viséed* by the Greek Consul then took me to the Italian authorities. We found our man in a big dingy room which was packed to suffocation with Greek, Corsican and Sicilian seamen and I suspected that they each and all lived exclusively on garlic.

Mr. Garguilo forced his way to the desk and talked a few minutes. The official looked over at me, stamped my passport, shook hands with Mr. Garguilo and turned again to his seamen. We got in Mr. White's car, which had been waiting, called at the hotel for my bags and went on board the steamer. Just as easy as that!

The boat was an awful tub and the accommodations were most primitive. The cabins were in pairs opening, one on each side, on tiny corridors which ran at intervals from the dining *salon*. In the cabins were two berths on the inner wall and one under the port hole. That was all. Not a chair or a wash basin or any other thing but just those three extremely uninviting berths. At the end of each corridor was a basin with two tall taps standing so high above it that they splashed all over the place whenever they were turned on. One day a beautiful little eel, about five inches long, came merrily through into my tooth-wash glass.

BULGARIAN DEAD

One could secure a little privacy by locking the door into the dining salon, but there was no guarantee that one's opposite neighbours would not want to wash and pounce out at inopportune moments. In the morning I managed by rising very early, and during the day I would watch until my neighbours were on deck, then lock the corridor door until I had had a soul-satisfying scrub.

The food was horrible and the service worse. We had terrific storms and there were frequent rumours of submarines—though how anyone could have detected their presence in such rough seas passes my comprehension.

At Patras we got the news of the flight of Mr. Venizelos to Crete and immediately the young Greeks on board were aflame with patriotism.

As has been often told, King Constantine of Greece had been more than suspected of playing a double game with the Allies. His former Prime Minister, Eleutherios Venizelos, great patriot and true friend of the Allies, had protested in vain against the secret pro-Germanism of the king's policy but in vain. The queen, a sister of the *Kaiser*, had a most malign influence over her husband and he was as wax in her hands. While King Constantine was assuring the Allies of his friendly neutrality, he was secretly corresponding with Wilhelm of Germany and assuring him that it was only fear of Allied pressure that restrained him from openly declaring his sympathy with the Central Powers.

Nearly every one of the Greek patriots on our ship left us to go by a vessel just about to leave the harbour, which would arrive in Athens a few hours before we should. They declared their intention of defying the king and aiding Mr. Venizelos in setting up a government which would insure the integrity of Greece and balk the Pro-German plot of the court. Many of these young men I afterwards saw in Salonika with the forces of the Provisional Government.

On arrival at Athens, we found the whole town humming with excitement. The guards around the palace were doubled and at all hours of the day and night small groups of cavalry would dash past the hotel or we would hear the shuffle and tramp of hoofs. Squads of French marines were marching through the principal streets and one night a mob threatened to stone the French Legation. No one was allowed to walk on the legation side of the street after that.

The first morning I was in Athens a friend said that if I would ask I could have an audience with the queen, but my cold was so bad that it seemed unwise to do so since I did not wish to court influenza. In the

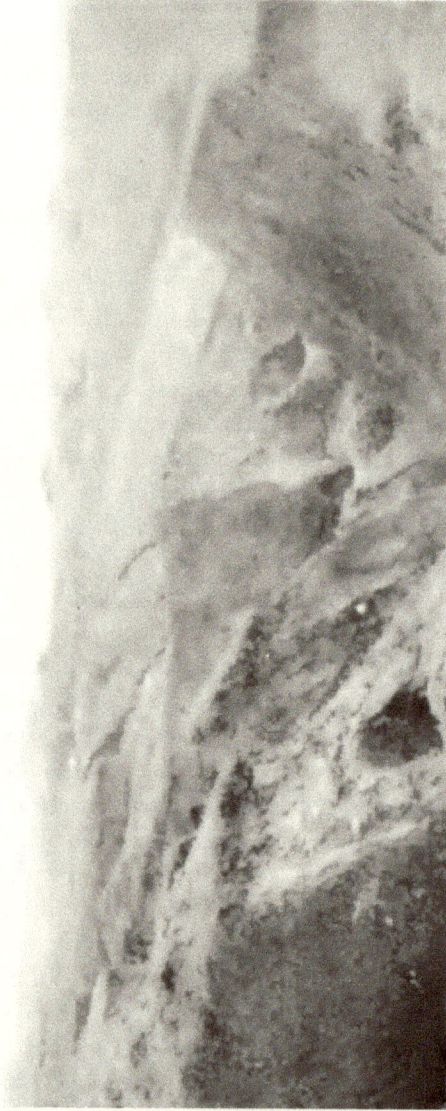

Bulgarian Trenches near Bród

afternoon a similar suggestion was made with regard to an interview with Princess Andrew, sister-in-law of the king, to which I gave the same excuse.

I hoped to see Mr. Venizelos and hear from his own lips the true state of affairs, if I could get to Salonika (I believe that it was well known in the Greek Court that I had no desire to see the queen before I did know the truth). The American Minister, Dr. Garrett-Droppers, assured me that this was impossible as Salonika was a "port of war" and entirely under military control. No person who was not actually engaged in some way in the conduct of the war, was supposed to be allowed to go there and the restrictions were very severe. However, he offered to introduce me to Sir Francis Elliott, the British Minister.

The interview was very short. Sir Francis seemed in a very nervous state, which was small wonder considering the heavy responsibilities devolving upon him. So after Dr. Droppers had told him my aims and wishes, I spoke up:

"Sir Francis, I know how busy you are and so I will not waste your time. If you can let me go say so, and if you cannot I'll just go away and try to be satisfied." The minister looked at me sharply a moment.

"We'll see what we can do," he replied.

Calling his secretary, he sent us down stairs to the Bureau des Allies. Here I filled in the usual application form and produced the perpetually required photographs. Then I was ushered out into the garden where a thick-set, youngish-looking man in a bowler hat, looked into my very soul and asked a few more questions. Then he asked Dr. Droppers something which I did not hear, and turning to me, said, "This passport must be *viséed* by the French, English, Italian and American Consuls here. That will take time but when it is done you may go to Salonika."

"I'll start on it now so as to sail tomorrow," I answered. Everybody laughed at my hurry and the official said:

"Well, if you are in such haste, I will attend to it for you. It will probably cost about fifteen *francs* in consular fees and I will send the passport around to you, in order, this evening."

I was amazed at his kindness, for everybody was rushed to death in Athens at that time owing to the unsettled state of Greek affairs and the very real danger to the legation from Anti-Venizelist mobs.

During my short stay in Athens I was much surprised at the very outspoken way in which the Greek situation was discussed by the

95

public. In restaurants, cafes, shops and hotels no one moderated his voice in commending Mr. Venizelos and criticising the king. I heard officers in uniform openly say that if Constantine did not come out plainly on the side of the Allies at once they would join the ex-premier in Salonika on his arrival there, which was expected to take place about ten days later.

The hairdresser at the hotel told mc gravely that Mr. Venizelos was "divine" and that his every word was "inspired by God." The man was intelligent and fairly well educated and said thousands of Athenians felt and believed as he did. I was much interested as I had heard both foreign residents and Greek officers say this was the popular feeling.

In the evening a messenger arrived with my passports. The next morning I spent at New Phaleron where I inspected the Frothingham Institute, an establishment where Serbian orphans were being cared for by the great generosity of John Frothingham of New York.

These children had been gathered from refugee camps where they were wandering forlorn and in terrible condition, having become separated from their parents. I was told that all had been in an extremely bad state when taken in charge by the institute. Then they were starved and ill, suffering from skin diseases, frost bites and various injuries.

But when I saw them they were well and looked happy, though on many of the little faces there were the ineffaceable traces of the suffering they had undergone. They filed before me, shaking hands solemnly, and saying in English, "How do you do." I had come prepared with a large box of sugared almonds, one of which I popped into each little mouth to the surprise and joy of the recipients.

Then the boys and girls stood in a group and sang the Serbian National Anthem and "Yankee Doodle came to town, riding *in* a ponee." Even the tiniest tot put up his little head, opened his wee mouth wide and sang out lustily.

While I was talking to the children one was referred to as "Our bad boy." The boy evidently understood what was said for he hung his head and looked very sheepish. Then they told me that one of his exploits within the past twenty-four hours had been to climb a telegraph pole in front of the institute and encourage the little boys to do the same until the poles from end to end of the road were draped with cheering Serbian orphans. And another of his pranks was to turn the tap of the big water reservoir to see the water splash and run away down the dusty garden. As all the water had to be brought by hand, this was quite a serious piece of mischief. However, I looked at him and said:

"I like bad boys for I believe that if a child knows he is bad he generally tries very hard to be good, and, if he tries hard enough he generally succeeds in laying the foundation of a good character and becomes a fine man—so I *do* like bad boys." This seemed a surprising point of view and all the children said they would *try* to be good! When I went away the children all stood on the steps and cheered lustily, "Hurrah for America."

At noon, Miss Simmonds, an American Red Cross nurse who has done wonderful work for the Serbians, joined me on board one of the small steamers and after many formalities we sailed.

There were three separate alarms of submarines the first day out. At every port we touched there were Venizelist demonstrations by the five hundred or more volunteers who sailed with us. At Volo feeling between our fellow-passengers and the townspeople ran high and shouts of "*Zito, Venizelos*" by those on board and the yells of opprobrium from the shore were deafening.

On deck the people were packed like sardines both day and night because few of the men took berths owing to the warm weather. My canvas deck-chair reeked with garlic after the first night, so I knew that some would-be warrior had slept in it. Miss Simmonds and I had been lucky enough to get a tiny cabin to ourselves,—so tiny that we had to dress in our bunks much as one does in a sleeping car. The food was very good and the boat scrupulously clean, which was explained by the fact that the owners are Scotch. These boats, and those of the Italian line by which I returned, were very enjoyable exceptions to the usual run of boats out there. The Greek vessels are simply abominable in every detail, of food, service and accommodation.

Miss Simmonds (or "Emmy Lou" as she was called by her intimates), Mr. Herbert Corey, the war correspondent, and Mr. Petchar, a Serbian Government official who had been charged to look after me by Mr. Balougditch, Serbian Minister to Greece, and I formed the party of four which generally managed to occupy the whole platform, and here we argued and gossiped and settled the Affairs of Nations to our heart's content.

Approaching Salonika, we had to wait some time for the examining officials to come on board and were much interested in watching life on a cruiser which lay close by. It was near sunset and the fishing boats were coming in. They were a lovely sight with their patched

Emily Louisa Simmons

sails shining like gold in the orange glow from the West and their hulls painted rosy pink, vivid green or deep maroon. Before us lay the curving line of buoys marking the guarded entrance to the harbour, and, rising across the bay, Eternal Olympus watching over all.

At the last moment we were allowed to enter—the entrance is closed at sunset—and I saw a different harbour from the one of a year earlier. It was now filled with war vessels, great battleships, cruisers, destroyers; tiny launches darted in and out; bugle calls floated over the water and the circling aeroplanes came slowly down the sky. A huge hydro-aeroplane swooped down to the surface of the bay like a monstrous dragon-fly, while, stately and beautiful in their pure white paint with the green band around their hulls and the great red cross painted on each side, lay the splendid ships, with their loads of sick and wounded men—the Hospital Ships. Two or three of these cleared daily for Malta, or France, or England, so great was the burden of sickness and wounds laid upon the "Armies of the Orient." Some of these vessels were attacked by submarines and, as we know, in several instances the Hun satisfied his blood-lust with the lives of these broken and suffering men and the nurses and doctors who tended them.

CROWN PRINCE'S HEADQUARTERS NEAR BRÓD

CHAPTER 15

Salonika

The harbour of Salonika when I arrived from Athens was crowded with Allied troops and all the paraphernalia of war.

A new Custom House and large, clean warehouses had been built since my last visit and ships were unloading stores, provisions, munitions, guns, ambulances, troops, hospital units and kicking mules in a seemingly inextricable jam. Mountains of baled hay were neatly stacked near the shore-end of the docks and bags of oats were piled up beside them. Lumber and mysterious cases filled another enormous space while winding in and out among the press came columns of troops looking fit for any work—or play!

The whole town was aflutter with the Allied flags now settling slowly down as night fell. My old room at the Olympos Palace was ready and friends came to call as a preceding boat had brought word that I *hoped* to come.

The town was clamorous with troops of a dozen nationalities and every shade of colour—English, French, Russians, Italians, Serbians, Annamese, Senegalese, Congolese, and American war correspondents bravely clad in tweed or khaki. There were nurses in white and blue and gray, doctors, surgeons and orderlies; Greeks, Jews, Serbians and Macedonian refugees. Every known language seemed to be spoken and every tint of the rainbow worn. It was like a tapestry of colour woven on a background of khaki and hung against the white walls of the old Thessalonian city.

I have been told that "women who ask questions" were particularly unwelcome to the authorities, so I set about my business very silently. The only questions I ever asked were absolutely concerned with my own work and I soon found plenty of that to occupy me.

First there were the American and Serbian Consuls to be seen. Mr.

Kehl, the American Consul, was far from cordial when I first saw him, and after a short conversation I could not blame him.

It appeared that various relief organisations in America, our own among them, had been sending goods out to Salonika "in care of the American Consul" with a calm request that these large boxes and bales should be forwarded to Nish or Monastir, or be distributed among the camps there in Salonika, but omitting to send funds for the freight or portage.

This, therefore, had to be paid out of the consul's own pocket, as the associations had no representatives on the spot to whom he could apply, and naturally the consul felt the imposition. It was, of course, merely lack of thought on, the part of those who had sent the goods, but when I promised to see that the matter should be corrected Mr. Kehl, who is only too glad to help in the good work, forgave us all and both he and Mrs. Kehl were very kind to me during my stay in Salonika. Then, accompanied by Miss Simmonds, I began the round of the hospitals and camps.

There were many pitiful sights and many more heart-breaking stories, but, on the whole, the poor refugees were comfortably housed in tents and wooden barracks and a school had been started for the children. Many of these had lost their parents or, in some cases, the parents were so dazed with the misery they had endured that the little ones were almost as badly off as if they were actually orphaned. Miss Simmonds was to take some of these children back to New Phaleron to be cared for by the Frothingham Institute.

In the tent wards of the Scottish Women's Hospitals I saw many Serbian soldiers and among them three old friends, soldiers who had been in Madam Grouitch's hospital in Belgrade three years before. They remembered me and called out feebly "*Sestro, Vinchestare!*" They had not forgotten that I had told them I had lived in Winchester and that the people there would send aid to the sick and suffering of Serbia.

In several other hospitals the Serbians were being cared for by the English and French and one day in the Place Liberté, I came face to face with that splendid woman, Dr. Rosalie Slaughter Morton. She had been warmly welcomed at Salonika and was invited to work with the French surgeons among the Serbian wounded.

My work in Salonika was to inspect the condition of the refugees in the camps and hospitals; to find out just what form of effort on the part of my committee in America would be most acceptable; to straighten out the questions of the forwarding of freight to different points by the kindness of the American Consuls and of funds for such forwarding, porterage, etc.; these last not the least important items since we were sending large quantities of foodstuffs and clothing as well as medical supplies. This took time for everybody was so busy that I often had to go several times to get a ten-minute interview with some man who really had not ten *seconds* to spare.

But I had not taken this long, dangerous and fearfully expensive trip to be balked by volumes of detail. So I inspected, investigated, questioned and worried everybody and everything that concerned Serbian Relief until my note-book was full and every vexed point had been covered and thoroughly cleared up.

When I started back to face my committee, if there was anything that I did not know about refugees or hospitals for Serbians or general relief in refugee camps, that thing was not worth discussing! My work was done.

Miss Simmonds, Mr. Corey and I used to desert the hotels and dine at the "Restaurant of the White Tower," where the food was excellent and the service passable. Here we would often invite one or two of the youthful British officers to join us for coffee and it was really touching to see how glad these lonely, home-sick boys were to talk with people of their "own kind." The nurses and doctors are, as a rule, too busy to talk to them unless they are ill and, though there was a large amount of feminine society to be found in the restaurants and concert halls, it was of a particularly undesirable type. On my return to England, I carried many messages to the parents of these young men and they were most appreciative of such "uncensored" news as I could give. I do not mean that I carried forbidden letters but oral messages which, brought by one who had talked recently with their dear sons, were very precious.

CHAPTER 16

Off to the Front

After I had completed my work in Serbia and was preparing to depart for England and America to continue the solicitation of funds for the Serbian cause, I was invited to call on Colonel Dr. Sondermayer, head of the Military Medical Service of the Serbian Army. In spite of his Teutonic sounding name the colonel is a true and patriotic Serb, but he speaks only Serbian and German. During my visit at his office, he happened to mention that he was going up to Ostrovo on the following day.

At this I started forward and said, "I'd give a year of my life for such an opportunity."

My work in Serbia prior to this time had been confined to hospital and administration work, both in the Bulgarian War and during the typhus epidemic at the beginning of the European War. And at this time I was about to return to the United States to continue the War Relief work on the lecture platform, which I had started the year before.

I had been at the front before in former years, and I had seen the war in all its severity but things had now changed. Serbia was for the moment not at bay. With the Allied aid she was actually driving the enemy back, back over the tortured country. Here was the chance to see Serbia regenerated, doggedly contesting every inch of the advance to her capital at Belgrade.

So when Colonel Sondermayer said he would take me with him on his next trip, I was quite unable to eat or sleep for excitement. It wasn't morbid curiosity. Heaven knows I had seen enough that was morbid in the three previous years. I wanted to see the Allied soldiers winning—driving back the enemy—victorious.

It was not until five days later, however, that Colonel Sondermayer dashed into the hotel with ; the demand "Can you be ready in half an hour?"

"Of course," I replied. In ten minutes Miss Simmonds had lent me a soldier's cap and other military paraphernalia. A Red Cross brassard was pinned on my arm and with a tooth brush, soap and not much else in a knitting bag, I was ready to go to the Front.

This was the inauspicious and particularly unimpressive way in which I started on my career as a soldier.

The town was jammed with people, as Mr. Venizelos was to arrive that day. The streets and houses were decorated with flags and wreaths of flowers; brilliant draperies flaunted from the windows and all wheel-traffic in the main streets was halted. We crept out of town through the narrowest back streets one ever imagined. Every soul in Macedonia seemed to be coming into town and it is little exaggeration to say that we were the only ones going out.

Our rattling Ford seemed to eat up the miles as we flashed past the English and French camps and over the level plains, with now and then a stone hut or a ruined cottage, an occasional shepherd or goatherd with their flocks and now and again a dead horse with a pack of wild dogs tearing and fighting over his thin carcass. There were little groups of gaunt unhappy-looking peasants squatting by the roadside or wearily plodding on toward the city. Some were Greeks, some were Macedonians, but many were obviously Serbians.

Just at sunset we came to a long ridge of low hills and on their slopes, blending with the earth and rocks in such a way as to be nearly invisible from a little distance, were the tents of the Serbian Escadrille. Colonel Sondermayer's son was stationed here. We stopped just long enough to wish him good-luck and went on our way.

Around the turn of the ridge we glimpsed a great tent hospital capable of holding a thousand men. Above it pegged, out on the slope and visible to aeroplanes for miles, was an enormous white expanse of canvas with a huge red cross in the middle. This hospital has been bombed by enemy airmen several times and a number of patients and others have been killed. *Kultur* is practised on the Eastern front as well as in France!

The moon came up and we started climbing. Trees and bushes began to stand out sharply in the silvery light and the sound of water rushing down the rocky crevices by the roadside told us that we were approaching Vodena, ("The Waters") a hill-town of great antiquity. The wall of rock rose higher on our right and on the left we could

COLONEL DOCTOR SONDERMAYER

now see the flash of a waterfall. Suddenly a turn in the road plunged us into a street—but such a street!

It was narrow and paved with rough stones over which we bounced and swayed perilously. On either side were low, open shops like those in any Eastern bazaar, trees often growing up through the overhanging eaves, the sides and counter hung and piled with bright-hued wares. For some reason there was a great quantity of vivid red cotton goods everywhere displayed, though I never saw any of it in use,—except as forming the great red crosses invariably pegged out on the ground near tent hospitals. Frequently in the middle of the street, which widened to allow traffic to pass, were great trees and an occasional public fountain with a rude drinking-trough for the animals.

Coming out into a broader street, we saw before us a dimly-lighted white building much more pretentious than any we had seen since leaving Salonika and here we got out of the car (to the great relief of our stiffened limbs) and entered a large room with a few tables scattered about and a long counter, or bar, at one side. There were several Serbian officers and a few civilians drinking coffee and talking excitedly and they told us that an enemy airplane had been detected approaching the town about an hour before, but it had veered away to the east without doing any damage. Everyone was wondering if it would return. A supper of coarse bread, rather "musty" fried eggs and beer was placed before us and we had, of course, the inevitable coffee, hot and syrupy as it is always served in the Balkans.

Then a grimy man, who seemed to be the proprietor, showed me up to a small room containing two beds of particularly uninviting aspect, a washstand with a very small jug and basin, no water, and a rickety chest of drawers with a mirror over it which distorted one's face into a most hideous grimace. On my demand for water, the man brought me a tin mug full (perhaps a quart), and a towel as thin as paper about eighteen inches square and with a very large hole in the middle of it!

With these facilities having somewhat removed the stains of travel, I prepared to retire.

At the earliest peep of day I was outside the hotel and glad to be there. Going around the corner where the colonel's window was, I whistled and in a moment there was a head out of every window except his. Just at that minute he appeared around the corner and seeing me he clapped his hand to his head and exclaimed, "Heavens, what a night!" and I gathered that he, too, had had his troubles.

THE WHITE TOWER, SALONIKA

As I absolutely refused to enter the place again we got the car and went up to the railroad station where some Serbian military map-makers had a camp; here we were most cordially received and had breakfast. Seated on soap-boxes we were served with bread, Scotch shortbread, goat's cheese and copiously-sweetened tea served in glasses.

It was all done so kindly and with such exquisite courtesy that the odd fare seemed to be the best one could possibly have and I shall long remember that hour spent at the camp at Vodena station while the sun cast a rosy glow on the distant mountains, and birds began to sing just as if there was no such thing as sorrow or mortal agony, nor half our world bathed in blood.

CHAPTER 17

"The American Unit"

After breakfast Colonel Sondermayer had to inspect a train-load of sick and wounded men who were on their way down to Salonika from the front. I went with him. Two Serbian ladies were distributing cigarettes and chocolate to the men who packed the train. The sick men sat on the seats with the worst cases lying across their knees or on the floor.

They were a pitiful sight. Even the longed-for cigarettes could not bring a smile—just a languid half salute and a murmured "*Fala.*" There was a constant stream of fever-stricken men being sent down at that time, though the Serbians stood the climate infinitely better than the French and English.

Just before the sun rose we packed ourselves into the Ford and started for Ostrovo. Passing again through the town, we stopped at a tobacco shop and bought out the stock of cigarettes, as we had heard that the wounded near the Front had been three days without them.

All the little shops were open and peasants were coming in with ox-wagons filled with straw and vegetables. An officer on horseback dashed up to the car, asked a question or two, saluted and galloped away. Sentries stepped forward, saw the uniform and red crosses, saluted and stepped back into their doorways. Rattling, bumping and skidding, we crept out of town and began our descent from Vodena.

The dust was deep and came up in clouds while the air before us was dim with it. A French soldier, in the gray-blue uniform, and with his steel helmet painted the same shade, sat panting by the roadside and ten yards further on we passed two more. Then rounding a rocky corner we came upon the rear guard of a column of French and Senegalese troops on their way to the Front.

We had to enter at the rear of this column and work our way

carefully through. It was exceedingly dangerous, both for us and for the soldiers, since the dust made it impossible to see anything more than ten feet ahead. We would crawl through the masses of men and dash past a huge "camion," only to pull up with a jerk to avoid an officer on a sweating, plunging horse, or a mule laden with bulging mysterious burdens closely covered with canvas and roped to the high pack-saddle.

The colonel was nearly strangled by the dust. He kept his handkerchief over mouth and nose, only removing it to shout to the men to make way. As he knew they would not understand Serbian he fell into the common error of thinking that his only foreign language would be more intelligible so used German!

Of course, the French soldiers, seeing our uniforms and brassards, and the red cross on the car, knew that we were all right, but the big Senegalese, hearing the "hated language," brought their rifles forward with a threatening gesture which made it necessary for me hastily to lean out and, in my very best French, beg them to please make way for "M. le Docteur *Serb.*"

These Senegalese were fine fellows and in their horizon-blue French uniform, with the "soup basin" steel helmet, were very formidable in appearance. They were a cheerful lot, joking and singing, in spite of the heat and dust which made their brown faces look like wet chocolate and their eyelashes and woolly hair resemble jute.

Their white teeth and eyeballs gleaming, they roared and rollicked along. I saw one jet-black, bullet-headed youth sitting by the roadside addressing a merry ditty to his big, blistered black foot while two others, roaring with laughter, prepared to soap the inside of his boot. The Frenchmen appeared full of nervous energy, though they did not sing or laugh. Often they saluted our cross and once or twice they gave us a hearty cheer, crying "*Vive la Serbia,*" as we passed.

At last we gained the head of the column and here a fine-looking French officer rode beside us for a time, asking questions. *Everybody* seemed to have the question habit except me! At last he left us with many good wishes and compliments on both sides. The country was now very beautiful and fine military roads were in process of being made. We often turned off on to the level turf to avoid a long stretch of newly-dumped road material, or places where the road bed had been excavated in preparation for it.

On our left were the long slopes of rolling hills and on the right a calm river with willows overhanging the water whence occasionally a few wild ducks, or a big blue heron would rise and fly away as we dashed by. If I often refer to our mode of progress as "dashing" it is because that exactly describes it. We would "dash" along at a good speed, hit a rock or a big hole, slow down a minute to make sure that our engine was still in its place, then "dash" on until we struck another obstacle!

After a couple of hours' ride, we halted before a gap in the low hills, which now lay on our right, and between them I saw a lovely sight. Imagine a group of white tents, with neat walks bordered by stones running before and between them, and in a large open space great trees spreading their branches over an altar before another, much larger tent; among them busy women in gray, or white, or khaki. Small ambulances stood in front of a white tent in the immediate foreground and nearby gossiped a little group of men who, I found, were convalescent Serbian soldiers acting as stretcher-bearers.

This was the American Unit of the Scottish Women's Hospitals[1] which had been established in Corsica with money raised by Miss Burke and myself in America in the spring. It had been removed from Corsica and set up at Ostrovo when the Serbian troops pushed northward and into their own country again.

The doctors, surgeons, nurses and ambulance drivers were all women and these latter were often young girls who had been brought up in the utmost luxury. But here they were, in khaki skirt, flannel shirt, heavy boots and with hair "bobbed" to save the trouble of dressing it, driving their cars up to the dressing station or to the railway, in sun, wind, or rain, by day or night, hopping down to do their own repairs or to "doctor" a balky engine. And all these devoted women had only one word of complaint—that they were not allowed to establish themselves nearer the firing line.

Their head was Dr. Bennett, a most efficient and capable person, a strict disciplinarian and possessing a particularly "British" personality. She came, I believe, from New Zealand, and the conduct of her hospital proved the highly executive ability of a voting woman! If American women only prove themselves as able in this war as the British women have done, the American men will have to look to their laurels at the polls or all the offices will soon be held by the newly-made "citizens."

---

1. *Scottish Nurses in the First World War*, a double edition, *With the Scottish Nurses in Roumania* by Yvonne Fitzroy and *A History of the Scottish Women's Hospitals* by Eva Shaw McLaren is also published by Leonaur.

I was shown through the immaculate wards of the hospital and distributed the cigarettes which we had bought at Vodena. It was touching to see how eagerly the men watched our approach. In many cases it was necessary for me to put the cigarette into the wounded man's mouth and light it for him. Then a box would be left between each two men to be shared by them. As we looked back from the door of each tent a feeble cheer of "*Givela Amerika*" followed us. At the entrance of one tent lay a dying man who, when he saw my basket, gasped, "*Sestro, cigarette.*" I put one in his mouth, lighted it; he drew a deep breath and died the happier because he had tobacco.

In another ward lay a young man not of the Serbian type. As I paused to put the cigarette into his mouth the nurse said, "He is a Bulgarian officer who was taken prisoner last night." The man, hearing the word, "Bulgarian," shrank from me and a look of defiance came into his eyes. But to any woman who has nursed wounded men, *any* injured man is only a poor boy, so I laid my hand on his forehead and smoothed back his hair. The tears came into his eyes and rolled down his pale cheeks. Then with his left hand he raised the coverlet and showed me the stump of his right arm. The nurse said that his right leg, too, was so mangled that they did not know whether they could save it.

Later in the day, the prince-regent, Alexander, made a tour of inspection through the hospital and when he came to this bed he asked the man if he was well treated there:

"Yes, Prince," said the Bulgar.

"Did you think you would receive kindness at our hands?" asked Prince Alexander:

"No, Prince," was the reply.

"Why not?" No answer.

"Is it because you treat our wounded and prisoners so cruelly?" demanded the prince. The man's face turned slowly crimson as he replied in a low voice, "Yes, Prince."

A Mass was held under the trees for the souls of the men who had died in that hospital. Prince Alexander, Prince George, Admiral Troubridge and a number of other distinguished officers, Serbian, French and English were present. The medical staff of the hospital stood facing the royal party, at right angles to the nurses and visitors. The tents made a background for the altar and the gorgeously vestmented priest, and a convalescent Serbian soldier served as acolyte.

It was an unforgettable scene, this little nook between the hills

MAJOR DOCTOR GELIBERT AT SALONIKA AND SURGEONS OF
SCOTTISH WOMAN'S HOSPITAL

only visible from the road directly before it or from the sky overhead, in which lay pain and sacrifice, death and life, fearless men and devoted women. Over us the red cross and the blue sky, in the soft air the smell of incense and solemn murmured words of prayer.

It was the first time Prince Alexander had visited this hospital and a luncheon had been prepared. The mess tent was decorated with flags in his honour and long white tables were placed along the sides. The prince-regent sat at the middle one with Dr. Bennett on his right and myself on his left. Beyond Dr. Bennett was Prince George and at my left sat Admiral Troubridge, a handsome white-haired Englishman who had distinguished himself by suddenly appearing by some mysterious route, on the Danube early in the war with a British gun boat, and who is now attached to Prince Alexander's Staff. Opposite was General Vassitch, Chief of Staff and Colonel Dr. Sondermayer.

The prince was most interested in hearing of my work in America and asked many questions as to America's attitude toward the war and especially toward Serbia. He urged me to tell my friends in America how deeply he appreciated what America had done, and was doing, for his suffering people and said he wished to see me in Salonika before I returned home that we might have a further talk.

"But, *Madame*, you must have seen many hospitals," he added. "If you want to see real war and conditions out here, why do you not go up nearer to the front?"

"Your Highness, I would like to go as far as possible," I replied. He spoke across the table to General Vassitch, who saluted, then turned to me.

"How far do you want to go?" he asked.

"Just as far as you will allow me," was my quick answer. They all laughed and Colonel Sondermayer got his instructions, which were to take me up to Old Vrbéni, the headquarters of Voivode Mishitch, commander-in-chief of the Serbian Army.

So my wildest hopes were realized. I was to see the battle front!

WOUNDED BEING BROUGHT IN ON MULE BACK

CHAPTER 18

Approaching the Battle Line

At this time the Serbians, French and English had succeeded in driving the enemy back as far as a place called Bröd on a very recent offensive. Here both sides had "dug in." The Serbian lines were just outside Bröd, while the enemy lines ran through the streets of this Serbian town. Thither we directed our course the day following my official permission.

The afternoon of my last day at the hospital was spent in climbing the hills around the hospital whence we could get glimpses of the town of Ostrovo and of the road leading away to the Front. Occasionally an ambulance would crawl out of the far hills and come down the winding road to the hospital. Now and again an aeroplane would float into view and circle about, reflected in the glassy mirror of the Lake of Ostrovo—and then suddenly dart away in the direction of Florina.

That evening Dr. Bennett, Colonel Sondermayer and I dined with General Vassitch in an upper room of a stone house in the ruined and almost deserted village nearby. The entrance was through a gap in a rough wall, then through a cobbled courtyard which had once evidently been a cow-byre, and up a flight of dangerously uneven stone steps. The room was roughly plastered but dazzlingly bright with fresh whitewash and around the rude table, which stretched from end to end of the place, were a most splendid lot of keen-eyed, bronzed, broad-shouldered Serbian officers.

The general sat at the head of the table. He was studying English and improved his opportunity by practicing it on us. He was reading Dickens, he told us, and he was most enthusiastic over it. Nearly all these officers spoke either French or German and conversation was as general as the long table would permit. Toasts were drunk in the light native wines, songs were sung and old campaigns fought over. It was a most exhilarating evening and I at last left the hospitable gathering and went out into the brilliant October night feeling that "*Life is full of a number of things*" and that it was given to me to share most fully in it.

I slept at the hospital that night, and having been assigned to the tent of an absent member of the unit, I was soon in bed—but, alas, I could not sleep.

A camp cot is a length of canvas on a frame, and if you know how to manage you *can* sleep on it with great comfort, but I did not have the necessary knowledge. There were plenty of warm covers that had been placed on the cot by kindly hands, but I felt nearly frozen. It was a very cold night and my coat and dress and a mackintosh which was in the tent were all piled on top of me by morning—and still I shivered. No one had thought to tell me—and I did not discover until too late to profit by it—that one must put something warm under one in a camp bed, else there is nothing between one and the chilly air but a sheet and one thickness of cold, hard canvas.

This was the second night of wakefulness, but dawn found me eager and ready for another long day of adventurous effort. After a hasty breakfast we bade the splendid women of the hospital goodbye and started again toward the sound of the guns.

Along the shores of the beautiful lake, with its tiny islands bathed in the rosy light of just-before-sunrise, through a valley of deep clogging sand and then a long ascent into the rocky hills over which our gallant Ford struggled and coughed and rattled and tugged. Sometimes we would have to wait, turned sidewise on some almost precipitous slope while the engine gathered itself together for some supreme effort to get us to the top. Once there, we slid and bounded and almost tumbled down over big stones and holes, only to begin another toilsome climb worse than the last.

We overtook and passed the French troops of our yesterday's meeting, but now they were seated by the roadside, having their morning meal, and they waved their steel helmets and cheered as we joggled by.

At the edge of a level plain the road branched away to the left to the French base at Florina, but we kept to the right until the road curved into a little ruined village—Old Vrbéni. From the moment we took the road at the fork the flat country had shown signs of the heavy fighting which had so recently taken place over all this territory.

Everywhere were rolls of cruel barbed-wire, neatly stacked shell cases and the baskets in which they are handled, broken rifles, scraps of metal and all the various debris of battle. The earth looked like rudely ploughed land, so pitted and torn with shell holes was it, and everywhere were the rude earthworks which had been thrown up by Serb and Bulgar. Sometimes these were a long line of mud embankments behind which many men could shelter; but more often the earth was scooped out in a tiny nest like a hare's "form." Some of these faced North and some South. There were many into which the earth had been roughly shovelled back and we knew that these held Bulgarian dead.

The Serbians were buried in plots of ground carefully marked off by rows of field stones; over the graves were small wooden crosses, new and shining—yellow like gold. When we passed one of these, my companions crossed themselves and I think we all offered up a silent prayer for brave men living who are fighting for all that is true and just on earth, for liberty and for peace; and for brave men dead, who had fallen for these glorious ideals.

Our car was turned through a gap in the hedge and we rolled into a level field. Before us we saw a tent into which stretchers holding motionless forms were being carried. This was the dressing station nearest to the Serbian line. Within the tent soldiers with their wounds dressed lay upon the bare ground, at best with only a handful of straw under them and still in their ragged and soiled uniforms.

There were no ambulances up there and the wounded were brought in from the battlefield on stretchers carried by two men. We saw also a curious contrivance of two large wheels with a sort of stretcher hung from the axles. This could be managed by one man, though as it jolted over the stony ground the wounded man would groan in agony. Every time a man would cry out Colonel Sondermayer would flinch and his eyes grow dark with pain. When he spoke to or examined men in the tents he was like a tender father. The soldiers adored him.

After half an hour we went on to an inn on the other side of the village, and here I was presented to the commander-in-chief of the Serbian Army, Voivode Mishitch. Not tall, rather lightly built, this wonderful soldier does not impress a stranger with a sense of power until one meets the full, direct look of his eyes. Then one sees that here is a man. Calm, impersonal, his look bores into one's inmost being, and I should not care to see him angry—*with me* at any rate.

He was much interested in hearing of my work and asked if I wanted to go yet nearer to the battle line. To my emphatic affirmative

VOIVODE MISHITCH, PROF. REISS AND LIEUT. PROSKOWETZ

he said, "We will see what can be done," and after we had had coffee. Major Todorovitch, his *aide-de-camp*, was sent for, given his instructions, and we bade the Voivode "*au revoir*," climbed into our faithful car and started again toward the roaring guns.

Just outside the village stood a group of captive Bulgarian officers, whose guards saluted us, grinning with triumph as we passed. About a mile further on we saw eight hundred or more Bulgarian prisoners in their earth-brown uniforms standing in groups by the roadside or bathing their feet in the ditch. The Serbian guards were sharing their scanty store of tobacco with these men and, remembering the horrors of the Bulgarians' treatment of Serbian prisoners and wounded upon the battlefield, I could only wonder at their charity.

In the almost demolished villages we saw ragged, haggard women winnowing corn, tossing it in the air with weary gestures, while near them sat the pale, emaciated children who had forgotten how to romp and play,—whose only thought now seemed to be "when shall we get something to eat?" I picked up a little child and tried to fondle her, but she shrank away and began to wail in a feeble, frightened way and I had to turn her over to her mother for comfort. Further along the road a little girl lying on the low bank smiled at me, but her yellow skin drawn over the sharp bones told a tragic story. I stopped the car and went back to see if I could do anything, but when I spoke to her she did not answer. I took her in my arms but she was already dead. "What was the trouble?" I asked.

"She was my child. She had great hunger," the mother replied simply. I gave the mother some cakes of chocolate, which was all I had with me, and some money, but the low voiced "*Fala*" of these wretched people was so hopeless that the tears ran down my face and I felt that my heart would break.

Now the road was over rough undulations of ground, brown and sterile in appearance and with low mountains rising before me. Suddenly Major Todorovitch turning, cried, "Look!'—and far up in the blue sky I saw a flash of silver as the sun glinted on a wire or a wing. Behind it in the clear air grew suddenly three tiny, fleecy puffs of cloud—then three more—and three more. The plane must have been "burning the wind," as it was not visible to us for more than five minutes altogether, and we had seen it as soon as it lifted over the mountains before us. It was a Serbian machine and the lovely, soft cloudlets were the deadly, exploding shrapnel with which the enemy batteries were pursuing it.

Richard Wainwright   Lieutenant Proskoertz   Emily Louisa Simmons

SERBIAN FIELD HOSPITAL AT VRBENI

Down the hillside came a string of mules, each laden with a sort of pack-saddle holding two rude chair-shaped structures and in one of these on either side sat a wounded man. Other wounded men began to meet us, some with roughly bound up heads and with streaks of dried blood on their faces; some with arms in improvised slings and one boy who limped by with a bandage around one leg and blood dripping from it to the dust.

Where two stones, rudely set in the earth, marked a boundary, Major Todorovitch saluted.

"*Madame*," he said, "I have the honour to inform you that you are the first woman of any nationality to enter reconquered Serbian territory." All this time the thunder of guns had been growing louder and louder and at last we halted on a little plateau on which were a number of small tents and a line of fine cavalry chargers. Half a dozen officers, French and Serbian, came out to meet us and were surprised to see a woman—and above all, a *foreign* woman,—there.

CHAPTER 19

The Battle

When we came in sight of the front line trenches, the officers pointed out a hill on No-Man's-Land, situated between the opposing lines. This hill had been selected as the Serbian Headquarters' Observation Post for the coming battle. I call it a hill, but it was really a small mountain, and the guns from both sides were considerably elevated to send their shells over it into the opposing lines.

I cannot say it was the safest place in the world to visit because a shell now and then does fall short. But this hill was "as far as possible," where I had wanted to go—and I went.

I was actually "over the top," though not just as one who has not been there imagines it. But there I was between the enemy and our own front line trenches, with shot and shell screaming over my head, with men dying just below and behind me, and only chance and a four-foot-high rock between me and death.

There were no barbed-wire entanglements erected before the trenches; in fact, they had only been recently occupied and the line consolidated. Cavalry had taken part in the war on the French Front lately only in the Cambrai attack, but in the Eastern Front cavalry was quite commonly used in conjunction with the artillery at all times.

At this time it was the intention of our party to go across a sheltered section of No-Man's-Land and up that steep hill on horses—but unfortunately I was not dressed for riding war-horses, so we all made the trip on foot. I don't know whether there is more glory in getting killed going "over the top" on horseback than on one's own feet—but we left the horses behind.

The officers were obliged to toil up in riding boots with spurs and with the stiff, high collar of the trim Serbian uniform closely hooked up to their chins. Up the steep, rocky mountain side Major Todorovitch was most gallant, trying to help me over the roughest places, but as the path was exceedingly narrow, I soon found it easier for both when we walked in single file.

The sun poured down upon us and a sultry Indian Summer haze spread over the valley below us. In the tiny village of Bee far down on our left the enemy shells were falling and the thunder of hidden guns near us was almost deafening. Someone handed me a big wad of cotton wool with which I stuffed my ears—just in time, for we suddenly rounded a corner and came upon a group of great guns in full action. They were shooting, with a high trajectory, over the crest of the mountain and their shells were falling in the village of Bröd, just opposite.

We were not yet at our destination, however, and after another fifteen minutes of strenuous climbing on the twisted path, we scrambled over a final stretch of slippery turf and found ourselves surrounded by a group of officers who had arrived there shortly before we did, and were sheltered under a great rock on the summit. Colonel Milovanovitch, commanding the Morava Division, Colonel Vemitch, commanding the First Cavalry Regiment, and a number of others were just about to take lunch and I was at once given a place at the table.

It was a curious experience. The thunder of the group of guns near us had now ceased, but the battle still raged on the plain below. After we were a little rested and refreshed, Colonel Milovanovitch said, "Would you like to see what is going on?"

"Yes," I replied, "let me see all there is to be seen."

The commander of the Serbians said, "Will you go further into Serbia than we have yet been, *Madame?*"

And I, wondering, said "Yes."

"Give me your hands," he said, "and lean out."

So, bending out over the valley from the brow of the precipice, I went, by the length of my own body, further into Beautiful Serbia than the soldiers had gone.

From the beginning of the war we have been told that *this* war is not spectacular: that the soldiers sit in their trenches and see nothing but the barbed wire in "No-Man's-Land" and an occasional bursting shell, or have to dodge a shower of "*whiz-bangs*" from an invisible enemy when the opposing trenches are not too far away. Interspersed with this not-too-exciting mode of warfare are the terrific artillery duels, the rolling clouds of poison gas, the fiendish jets of liquid fire and then, mercifully, "over the top," and vengeance wreaked upon the enemy with the cold steel. Therefore, when we approached the line of battle, I did not in the least know which phase I would see—I *hoped* to see it all!

Under shelter of the rock they led me to the brink of a precipice and here I was able to stand between two great out-cropping leaves of stone, while I gazed at a battlefield spread in relief below. Level with the face of the precipice, and of course far below my eyrie, were the Serbian trenches with the big guns some distance behind them and the village, of which mention already has been made, some distance away on their left.

Every now and then a Bulgarian shell would fall among the little red-tiled houses and a cloud of dust and whirling leaves would rise, circle about and slowly settle. Once a riderless horse galloped out and then a stretcher was carried slowly away toward the dressing station—then another and another. From the mountains still further to the left, which run like a great spine from Florina to Monastir and sweep round beyond in a rocky curve, came the great shells from the French guns and the white and dun clouds of vapour from the explosions formed constantly drifting veils over the tortured valley.

On our right the Czerna River emerged from the mountains and flowed gently away into the hills again, and just in the elbow of the stream—the famous Czerna Bend—lay the village of Bröd. In it Bulgarians swarmed, while their artillery roared spitefully just behind a low, rounded hill near the town. With the binoculars I could make out the earth-brown figures of the soldiers and the line of a trench. Before us in the distance, like a cluster of pearls against the dark mountains, lay Monastir, nine miles and in the milling progress of the Allies, five weeks away!

The view from the Observation Post was more thrilling than anything I had anticipated. First of all there were few clouds of smoke to obscure our view and we were high enough above the battlefield to see all of it at once. Even the Bulgarian trenches across the river lay open to our view, and with the glasses I could see their guns slide forward, smoke belching from their mouths, and then settle back, while a moment later the *boom-m* of the explosion would come dully to my ears. Then the shell would burst over, or near, the trenches below me and I would turn my eyes away from the welter of maimed and bloody forms below.

Once I saw a group of men, perhaps eight of them, mashed to a gory pulp by three shells which fell close together in the Serbian line,

126

and a man close by who had apparently been untouched, but suffered a temporary derangement due possibly to tortured nerves, sprang out of the trench and, shaking his fists in the direction of the enemy, rushed blindly forward toward the river, into which he plunged and was lost to view.

Still dazed and gasping, I heard Colonel Milovanovitch ask, "Would you like to give the signal for our guns to recommence firing?" and, shaking with emotion, I nodded assent.

So, in the name of American Womanhood, I gave the signal which sent shells roaring over the valley to fall in the Bulgarian trenches. And the men behind me shouted "*Givela Amerika!*"

I was shaking from head to foot with excitement and the lust of battle. Major Todorovitch spoke,—

"Calm yourself, *Madame*; they have not just got our range up here yet. When it grows *too* dangerous we will take you away."

"Do you think I am afraid?" I cried. "I never *lived* before!"

CHAPTER 20

How I Became a Soldier

They may not have had our range on that hill—that is, the snipers did not; but it doesn't take heavy artillery long to get the range of the top of a hill in No Man's Land. The shells were constantly coming closer—those shells which I had just seen blow to pieces dozens of our brave allies. Yet, I can truthfully say, I was not afraid.

It has been said that "*Fools rush in where angels fear to tread,*" Perhaps this was my case, but it was all too thrilling—a wonderful experience—and I could not tear myself away.

The commander-in-chief stepped up to me while the battle was at its height.

"Haven't you had enough of it yet?" he asked.

"No, Excellency," was my reply.

"Well you should have been a soldier," he said.

"Make me one," I promptly responded. The colonel of the First Cavalry Regiment instantly put in his word.

"I want her to be made a member of my regiment," said he. And so, with the shells screaming over our heads at the most exciting moment of my life on that famous battlefield of Bröd, in October, 1916, I was made a member of the First Cavalry Regiment of the Royal Serbian Army.

I was no longer a woman helper. I was now a soldier, and, as I write this,—the only American woman soldier in this great war.

After my return to America, a large parcel containing the peculiar cloth of the uniform of the Serbian officer arrived, with the beautiful enamel "*Cocarde*" which is worn on the cap of every Serbian officer. No honour which Serbia could bestow upon me could make me so proud as the right to wear this uniform, which has been rendered glorious by those heroic men who so long and so bravely have fought,

From a photograph taken during the battle of Kirsi

Commander-in-Chief Voïvode Mishitch, Com. of Morava Div. Col. Milovanovitch, Chief of Medical Service Col. Dr. Sondermeyer and the author

and continue to fight, against such fearful odds and whose gentleness and patience under suffering have won the affection and admiration of every person who has worked among them.

I was allowed to remain in my rocky nook until night began to fall and then was told to return to the dressing station and wait.

"For what?" I asked, and the commander said that he believed that I had brought them luck and they would try to cross the Czerna that night.

"You will let me know when you make the advance," I begged.

There was a certain grim humour in my companion's eye as he said, "You'll hear us." And then I had to go. Down the mountain and over the plains, passing stretchers on which lay shattered bodies and from which, often, bright blood trickled down into the dust. An unlucky stumble by a stretcher-bearer would cause a quickly stifled moan from pale lips, and occasionally a brown hand would be lifted to a bandaged head in salute as we passed.

Arriving again at Old Vrbéni, the hospital staff greeted us cordially and gave a cheer when they were told where I had been.

"We hoped that you would be with us at luncheon and arranged to give you a real American dish but as you did not come we will have it prepared for your dinner," said the chief surgeon.

Now these brave men were living on the coarsest and scantiest of food and the country was denuded of everything, practically, so I wondered what they could have found for me. After a sketchy wash-up we sat down, with me at the head of the table were the higher officers, within the mess tent, and the younger ones at the other end, which extended outside. The lights were dim, flaring oil lamps and the tables were rough boards on trestles. There was a heavy hand-woven linen cloth at our end and clean paper spread over the places of the lesser officers at the other. We had two Frenchmen with us, one a great doctor and the other a young officer, just convalescent, who sat silent and brooding all through dinner.

Such a dinner! In our ears sounded the crash and roar of battle, and the moans of dying men. Sometimes a man in the hospital tent behind us would break into awful, hopeless sobbing and this would be checked by the choking cough, or horrid rattle, which told its own story of a soul passing into Eternity. Around our dimly lit table were surgeons, kindly-eyed doctors, bronzed officers with gleaming orders on their breasts; and I felt my high privilege to be sitting there with men who had given all, dared all, and were prepared to suffer all for

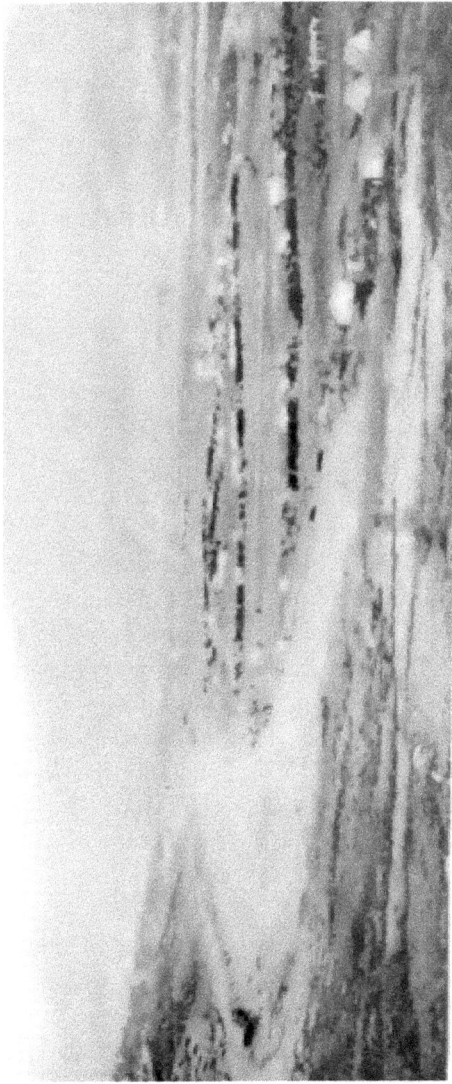

CZERNA BEND, FROM H.Q.O.P.

their country and her honour.

The "American dish" was served with much ceremony—a beautifully prepared platter of ham and eggs! Can you imagine how I felt?—to sit there and eat this savoury food when the gallant gentlemen who entertained me for weeks past had tasted nothing better than coarse broad and stringy goat's-flesh! My throat rebelled at every delicious morsel, but to refuse would have been not only to give pain but to offer a deadly insult to these proud men who hold nothing to be too good for their guests and no sacrifice too great for any who befriend them.

After dinner the younger men played on guitars and sang haunting melodies and stirring war-songs. A peasant soldier who was brought in read three poems of his own composition. At ease, and without a trace of embarrassment, he took the seat placed for him near the least smoky lamp and in a clear, musical voice, he recited a wonderful epic poem, which told how the Crown Prince Alexander, when stricken by illness on the awful march through the snow-filled passes of the Albanian mountains, refused to leave his men in order to gain comfort and safety more quickly.

"No," he replied to their entreaties, "I belong to you and my place is here."

The pride of the king in his noble son and the love of the suffering people for them both were eulogized. Next he read a stirring battle song and finished with an exquisite Song of Home, telling of the love of the soldier for his little white-walled dwelling with its fields of grain, its fruit trees, flocks and flowers; the courage of the chaste, deep-bosomed women and the laughing, fiery-spirited children. When he had finished each officer shook his hand and then he turned to me, with a true poet's look in his blue eyes, and said, "I kiss the lady's hand for our kind sister America." He raised my hand to his lips and, saluting, went out to join the reserves who were on their .way to the trenches.

Just as the singers began another plaintive melody, there came a sudden lull in the sound of the fighting. Then, sounding surprisingly near in the keen autumn night air, came an outburst of cheering when with a renewed thunder of the big guns doubling their fury, the cracking of machine guns and the occasional bursting crash of bombs, the Serbian heroes left their trenches, dashed across the stretch of open plain and crossed the Czerna River for the first time in their advance to Monastir. They drove the Bulgarians out, captured or killed hundreds and occupied the village of Bröd;—while we, back there in the ruined village of Old Vrbéni, cheered and sang and prayed for those who fought and won and those who suffered and died in the moonlight on the soil of their loved Serbia. As the stretchers came in with their piteous burdens they were greeted with triumphant songs of victory, and even men whose life blood was staining the shrivelled grass at our feet, found strength to mutter "*Givela Serbia*" before their eyes closed forever. My own soul was filled with an amazing sense of glory and my own country seemed more dear than ever before,—seeing what men could do for their native land,—and I sang "America" in a broken and sadly unmusical voice, but with all my heart in the words, while all those *blessed, blessed* men took up the air and at the end shouted again and again, "*Givela, Givela, Amerika.*" Whatever the years may bring to us, never again can I feel that Life has cheated me, for in these moments I *lived* and the memory will be mine forever.

At last the doctor insisted that I must get some rest, so I was put into a tiny tent in which a great bunch of belated marigolds had been placed, but there was not room for the flowers and me, and so they had to be put under the bed until I was in it, when I brought them out and propped them again against the canvas wall. When at last sleep came, it was only in fitful snatches, for the sound of the fighting, mingled with the low murmurs of the wounded men in their wards near me, kept my mind full of the excitement and exultation which had marked the day.

For the next five weeks there was continual fighting and gradually the Allied troops pushed the enemy back with fearful losses on both sides. Finally Monastir was recaptured and our troops entered the city amid the happy tears and rejoicing of the people. But the story of that advance, with its wake of blood, is not a pleasant thing to describe. It was war in all its horror, all its brutality, all its glory. Serbia's troops are only a little beyond Monastir today. The battle-lines are still drawn there. There is a dead-lock on the Eastern Front.

Perhaps, (as at 1918), the Teutons will make another attempt to push us out of Serbia. They will not succeed. The Allied Armies must hold that Eastern gate against all odds.

I might have gone back this Spring, but General Rashitch, when he was here with the Serbian Mission in January, said to me, "My sergeant, your duty to Serbia is here, pleading her Cause. You can do so much good here that I assign you to this work until further orders."

CHAPTER 21

The Return

When I started back again to America from the battle front to help the Serbian cause it was with mixed feelings since every atom of my being was crying out to remain with the Serbian troops. I met Colonel Sondermayer again at the little town of Old Vrbéni, whence I had previously started for the scene of battle.

We planned to get under way on our return to Salonika at dawn. After my night's sleep in the hospital tent, as the first glimmer of daybreak appeared, I was ready.

And here arose a difficulty. The orderly who the night before had laced the flaps of the tent—first the inner and then the outer one—had done it so securely that I was unable to get at the knots which were, of course, on the outside and there was nothing in the tent with which I could cut the cords. Outside Colonel Sondermayer stamped up and down, growling about women being always late, and there was I, ready even to my gloves, trying to make him hear so that he might let mo out! He was making so much noise himself that it was some time before my despairing cries could be heard, but at last he did hear and I was soon free.

We had a hasty cup of coffee and a slice of toasted bread and started back to Ostrovo. Along the road we met troops marching up to their bases, but were so fortunate as not to get caught in another column. There were little groups of ragged refugees straggling up the road and on one rocky stretch of break-neck descent we passed a recklessly bounding car from which the long arm of Prince George waved us enthusiastic greeting. The car flashed past us with such speed that all we could hear of his vociferous shouts was, "*A la bonheur*," and he was gone. An American nurse in Salonika told me that the nickname of His Highness' chauffeur was "The Lightning Conductor," because of his invariably speedy progress. Remembering his uproarious passing, I suggested that his *car* might be called "The Stormy Petrol."

Again the beautiful Lake of Ostrovo and the ruined stone village where we had dined—how long ago was it? Counting by *days* only two; counting by emotions, experiences, feelings, at least a year! We drew up at the gap in the hills before the Scottish Women's Hospital and soon were talking "fourteen to the dozen" to Dr. Bennett, who left her work to greet us. Our time was so short and we had so much to discuss that it was only after I was again in the car and Joko had cranked up that I remembered the most personal thing of all and shouted above the din of the car, "I was the very first woman of any nationality to enter re-conquered Serbian territory." She waved a friendly hand and called "Bravo" as we turned into the road and began our journey to Salonika.

Through the long, lovely valleys again, luncheon of bread and goat's-cheese on a rock by the smooth flowing river which furnished our only drink, then around the foot of the hill on which stood Vodena of uneasy memories. Again, we pulled up before the low stone huts and dun-coloured tents of the Serbian Escadrille. Tadoya, Colonel Sondermayer's son, came to escort us to the mess tent.

Oh, the heat under that canvas top, "camouflaged" though it was with green boughs! And the young enthusiasm of the youthful aviators for their perilous work! They laughed and sang and joked and called me "*Mon collegue*" until, middle-aged as I am, I began to feel that perhaps the thin red wine which we were drinking might actually be "the Elixir of Life"; and when I found myself singing "Tit Willow" for them, I just knew it! After this cheerful interlude we started again toward Salonika and at sunset our Ford rolled along the quay beside a Russian regiment which had just disembarked. Mr. Venizelos had arrived, amid great rejoicing, and was comfortably installed in a fine villa about two miles from the centre of the town, where he was, I suppose, the very busiest man in Salonika.

With him had come Captain George Melas, an old friend of mine with whom Miss Simmonds and I dined that evening. A formal dinner was being given to Mr. Venizelos in the "Concert Room" of the White Tower restaurant and the lobbies were full of Cretan guards, in their funny trousers and "pill-box" caps; eagle-eyed detectives and friends of the great man were in attendance too.

After dinner Captain Melas asked if I would like to see Mr. Venizelos, and I eagerly assented. So, with all the frock-coated and uniformed guards bowing and saluting at sight of our escort, we passed into the room behind a line of palms and up a tiny staircase to the boxes. But, alas, the only unlocked door was that of the box directly over the places of honour and we could only see most of the, to us, uninteresting three or four hundred other men. Some of them jauntily raised their glasses when they saw us appear, but this failed to amuse us and we descended to our little alley behind the palms on our way out. Just as we got halfway to the door, a gentleman with glasses and a short white beard turned from the table and looked directly at me. In an instant I recognised Mr. Venizelos, but then, a trifle panic-stricken at being caught staring, I scuttled out.

At eight o'clock the next morning Captain Melas came and told me that Mr. Venizelos would be pleased to see me at nine. In a flurry of anxiety as to whether he would give the order of "Off with her head," I set out with Miss Simmonds. It was a lovely autumn morning and the white villa, set in its garden of palms and late flowers, looked very beautiful but hardly peaceful, as the Cretan guards, armed to the teeth, stood at the gate and among the trees while detectives prowled in the streets and around all the corners. We went up the broad marble steps and in the hall found groups of earnest and solemn personages waiting their turn with the distinguished man. Everybody made way respectfully for Captain Melas and we were received by General d'Anglis and the Greek naval hero, Admiral Conduriotos.

After a few minutes the people who were with Mr. Venizelos came out and we were at once shown into the room. This room was open to observation from the hall, one side being completely glazed, so fearful were his friends that he might be attacked and injured. He greeted us most cordially

"Madame, I find Ingleesh veery deeficult—if you permit me French?" was his apology at meeting. Then for over an hour this, the busiest man in Greece at that time, talked with me of his plans and aspirations! He spoke of the king and said he hoped Constantine would see his way to come out openly on the side of the Allies "even now," and that in any case his own duty was clear. He gave messages for the Greeks in America, saying that it was their duty to return and fight with their Balkan Ally.

"We Greeks and the Serbians are natural friends and we must stand together," he said. "Tell them that they must help now for the honour of Greece and for her safety." In America I have given this message repeatedly in my lectures but have had no means of knowing if these

ELEUTHERIOS VENIZELOS, GREEK PREMIER

noble words have borne fruit.

Mr. Venizelos is a man of middle height, neither stout nor thin. His fine forehead is surmounted by nearly snow-white hair and a well-kept moustache and short beard shade his always smiling mouth and firm chin, but it is the clear blue eyes with their direct and honest gaze which hold one's attention from the first moment one meets him. One feels that here is a man, clean, sincere and strong. Before we parted he smilingly said, with a twinkle in his eye, "But, *Madame*, I am sure that I have seen you before."

"Yes, Excellency," was my reply. "Miss Simmonds and I were the only ladies present at your banquet last night and when you turned your head I lost mine." He seemed greatly amused. Then he signed two photographs which he gave to Miss Simmonds and myself and, despite the evident agitation of his friends and bodyguards, came out to the top of the steps with us to say goodbye. It was dangerous, too, for any miscreant waiting an opportunity could have shot him from the street as he stood there calmly talking.

"How warm the beautiful sunshine is today," he remarked.

"Excellency," I answered, "may you stand always in the sunshine."

"Ah, *Madame*," he said, "who can tell. But, sun or shadow, I know my way."

We went away feeling that we had seen history in the making—as indeed we had, and I do believe that while the affairs of Greece are in the hands of this splendid patriot, she will go far toward regaining some measure of her old glory.

The next day my ship was due to sail, so I went to the provost marshal to get permission to leave as this would save the endless round of the Allied Consulates, which is usually required. The provost marshal proved to be an old acquaintance whom I had not seen for many years, so we had a good talk. When I rose to go, he said, "Do you know we all know you here as the 'Woman Who Asks No Question and Attends to Her Own Business.'" I laughed, gathered up my documents and went away feeling that my extreme self-restraint had not been in vain!

A visit to Mrs. Kehl that afternoon, a farewell dinner at the White Tower and, later in the evening. Colonel Joannu, famous Greek soldier and Venizelist supporter, came in and, when several Serbian officers joined us, we had an international "*conversazione*" in which the affairs of many nations were discussed and settled to our own complete satisfaction.

VODENA

On the day set for my departure, the French officers and doctors at "Aviation" again invited me to lunch and Colonel Sondermayer arranged to call for me just in time for the boat. When he came he was so flurried that I was sure I had missed it, but when we turned off the main road into the Grande Quartier Serbe I said, "Well, if we ramble all over town *of course* we will be late." The colonel just sputtered and exclaimed fiercely, "Don't you know that Prince Alexander has been waiting hours to see you?" It was the first I had heard of it, but naturally I was pleased with the prospect of seeing the prince before leaving.

We arrived at the "palace," a great rambling villa in a garden with a tall fence and with picturesque Serbian guards at the gates and along the paths. An immaculate officer greeted us at the door and at the top of the marble staircase a frock-coated *major-domo*, bowing, met us. In a small irregularly shaped room, panelled in brocade and filled with French furniture, we waited and in a few moments Prince Alexander came to us. He is of medium height, well-built and erect, with a warm olive complexion and handsome dark eyes behind powerful glasses, a direct earnest gaze and a resolute manner. He seems older than his actual years and will, we all believe, be a splendid king when the time comes for him to take his place upon the throne of that Greater Serbia which the future will bring to stand as a strong sentinel in Eastern Europe.

For an hour we talked of Serbia and what America has tried to do for her and of what the Serbian Relief Committees are trying to do. The prince expressed his deep appreciation and said he had hoped the seeds and farming implements might be sent into the country the moment the war is over so that the people may plant and reap a good harvest.

"And," he added, "when the people have gathered their first crops they will ask aid of no one." But *we*, who have seen, know how much there must be done in sanitary and other matters—though the people will not ask.

"You wear two of our decorations, I see. I want you to wear a third in token of our gratitude for all your devotion to our cause," said the prince, leaning toward me. He held toward me the little blue and gold box which contains the coveted Order of St. Sava!

I was surprised and could only stammer, "Does Your Highness think I merit it?"

Then Prince Alexander pinned the Order on I my coat saying, "I know no better friend of Serbia than Ruth Farnam." After a few moments, he said, "You will return soon to help us in Monastir, will you not, *Madame?*" I explained that my services would probably be much more valuable in raising funds in America which would enable the trained workers to do their work out there.

"But, I will come back to go with the army into Belgrade!" I promised, and the prince replied that he should hold that as a promise. We shook hands, and I fled for the steamer.

The steamer was waiting for me and there was a brilliant gathering of officers and officials on board. Some were former office holders, under King Constantine, now displaced by the Provisional Government of Mr. Venizelos; and several were people who had come to see me off. There was a great deal of congratulation over my new Order and many messages given for friends in Athens and Paris, London and New York, all of which I tried to store into a head which was fairly whirling with excitement.

Soon the whistle blew and our friends left us, remaining on the water in the little boats until our ship was well away from the anchorage, and even then their shouts came faintly over the water as we moved out past the war vessels; past the great white hospital ships and toward the barrier of nets and mines guarding the mouth of the harbour. Many of our passengers were happily on their way to France or England on leave, but *I* regretted every mile which took me away from the white city and the wonderful men and women who were striving there to win freedom and to soothe the wounds of a tortured world.

If in these pages I have said little of the splendid women–nurses, doctors and surgeons who were devotedly working in Salonika and nearer the Front, it is not because I did not see them and their superb accomplishment but because no words of mine could do justice to them all.

There was our famous Dr. Rosalie Slaughter Morton, who chose to spend her hard earned holiday out there helping to restore Serbian heroes to life and hope. She made many an American heart beat faster with pride in American womanhood. Another hard working person was the Princess Demidov. There were Madame de Reinach-Foussemague, Dr. Honoria Keer, surgeon in the Scottish Women's Hospital, great little Dr. Alice Hutchinson, Mrs. Harley, the sister of General French, and who recently was killed by an exploding shell in Monastir; Dr. Bennett, and a hundred more, every one of whose names will be written in letters of gold in the memories of men for their heroic service and splendid devotion.

But of all these, we Americans must remember with pride the name of Emily Louisa Simmonds, an American Red Cross nurse, of British birth. She was one of the most devoted of the noble and gallant band who suffered and toiled untiringly and ungrudgingly for Serbia.

Arriving again at Athens, I found the city in a turmoil, with Allied troops—but mostly French marines—marching continually in the streets. There would be a sharp bugle-call and from every direction little Greek soldiers would run across the park before the hotel and line up under the trees. Officers with their clanking swords banging on their horses' sides would gallop back and forth and one lived in momentary expectation of an international explosion. Many of the officers with whom I had talked during my last visit had gone to Salonika, and every boat clearing from Piraeus took dozens of recruits. I remembered Mr. Venizelos' words to me:

We are the natural friends of Serbia. Her sorrows concern us and we must take our stand beside her now and always.

There were still Greeks who were loyal to the Janus-faced king, but even they were complaining of conditions in the country. Princess Andrew sent for me and I went to the palace. Before her marriage she was beautiful Princess Alice of Battenberg and her spouse was the brother of the king.

She certainly was not pro-German but was entirely pro-Greek, and since her sympathies were all with Constantine, one can only conclude that she did not in the least understand the true state of affairs. She was anxious to get me to work in America for the Queen's Refugee and Hospital funds. This I readily promised to do, if it would not clash with my work for Serbia, but was told later that these affairs were run in a rather haphazard way. Her Majesty not being quite as efficient as her German training would indicate.

On my return to America I spoke to several people about giving such time as I could to this work but met with little response.

My calls upon the Legations, American, French, English and Serbian, took up some time, but on the second day I left for Marseilles and, arriving in Paris early one morning, left the same day for Boulogne and London. The journey was long and extremely tedious, but as there was a convalescent French officer in our crowded compartment who grew paler and paler and at last asked permission to lie on the floor (among our feet!), no one felt like complaining over his own little troubles. Two men and myself then stood in the corridor, in spite of the Frenchman's protestations, so he had room to rest in comparative comfort. At the "town" station an Englishman met him, helped him carefully into a cab and they drove quickly off into the darkness.

The Channel boat was packed with travellers and we made the trip in utter darkness, as submarines were prowling about. Occasionally we would see a white gleam in the distance which must have been, we all believed, the "wash" of our guardian, an English destroyer, but the night passed without any untoward happening and just as the sun rose we landed on English shores.

A few days later I set sail for America to continue my work on the lecture platform and otherwise to help the Allied cause.

An English Woman–Sergeant
in the Serbian Army

COLONEL MILITCH, COMMANDANT OF THE SECOND REGIMENT
(ON THE LEFT)
AND HIS CHIEF OF STAFF; WITH THE REGIMENTAL FLAG.

Contents

Introduction

Innumerable have been the manifestations of sympathy, generosity, and of the sincere desire to help Serbia given by the British people to their little Ally since the very beginning of the war. No words could ever express the deep gratitude of the Serbian Nation for the splendid services rendered by the many British Medical Missions, whose staffs, men and women, have nursed the sick and wounded without a thought for the hardships and dangers to which they have been personally exposed, and which, especially during the typhus epidemic and, later on, during the Great Retreat, were very serious indeed. British women have played a most prominent part in this humanitarian work of charity and mercy, and some of them have even given their lives for the Cause.

When the history of their splendid achievements is written—as I hope will be done some day—the name of Miss Flora Sandes will certainly figure in it with a special acknowledgment. In the interesting pages which follow she will herself give a vivid description of her experiences during the Retreat in the ranks of the Serbian Army, in which, I believe, she was the only foreign woman allowed to serve in a fighting capacity. That in itself speaks very highly of the esteem and confidence in which she is held in Serbia. But she only took to a rifle when there was no more nursing to be done, as, owing to the army retreating, the wounded could not be picked up and had to be left behind. Before that she had worked in Serbia for eighteen months as a voluntary nurse, practically without interruption, having left the country but twice, and that on a short visit to London to collect funds and bring back with her dressings and other hospital supplies which were badly wanted. During the typhus epidemic she volunteered to go to Valjevo, which was the centre of the disease and where eight Serbian doctors and many nurses had already succumbed. The same fate very nearly overtook her, but fortunately she recovered and resumed immediately her self-imposed duty.

Such examples of self-sacrifice, added to so many others given by British men and women in Serbia, have implanted in the hearts of the Serbians a deep love and admiration for Great Britain, who may well be proud of such sons and daughters.

Slavko Y. Grouitch,
Secrétaire-Général of the
Serbian Ministry of Foreign Affairs.

CHAPTER 1

Rejoining The Serbians, November, 1915

Events moved so rapidly in Serbia after the Bulgarians declared war that when I reached Salonica last winter I found it full of nurses and doctors who had been home on leave and who had gone out there to rejoin their various British hospital units, only to find themselves unable to get up into the country.

I had been home for a holiday after working in Serbian hospitals since the very beginning of the war, but when things began to look so serious again I hurried back to Serbia. We had rather an eventful voyage, as the French boat I was on was carrying ammunition as well as passengers, and the submarines seemed to make a dead set at us. At Malta we were held up for three days, waiting for the coast to clear. The third night I had been dining ashore, and on getting back to the boat, about eleven, found the military police in charge, and the ship and all the passengers being searched for a spy and some missing documents. We were not allowed to go down to our cabins until they had been thoroughly ransacked, but as nothing incriminating was found we eventually proceeded on our way, with a torpedo-destroyer on either side of us as an escort.

The boats were always slung out in readiness, and we were cautioned never to lose sight of our life-belts. We had to put in again at Piraeus, and again at Lemnos for a few days, so that it was November 3rd before we finally reached Salonica—having taken fourteen days from Marseilles—only to find that the railway line had been cut, and there was no possible way of getting up into Serbia. My intention had been to go back into my old Serbian hospital at Valjevo to work under the Serbian Red Cross as I did before; that was out of the question now, of course, as Valjevo was already in the hands of the Austrians, but I thought I might get up to Nish and get my orders from the President of the Serbian Red Cross there. I inquired from a Serbian officer staying at the hotel, who had just ridden down from Prisren, if it would be possible to ride up into Serbia, but he most strongly discouraged all idea of riding, saying that with every facility at his disposal, and relays of fresh horses all along the route, it had taken him ten days to ride from Prisren to Salonica, and that during that time he had frequently been unable to obtain food either for himself or his horses; that, furthermore, it was very dangerous even with an escort, as part of the way was through hostile Albania, and that all the horses were needed for the army. I gave up that idea, therefore, and set to work to find out where I could come into touch with the Serbians, and finally found I could go to Monastir, or, to call it by its Serbian name, Bitol. Accordingly, I, with four other nurses and a doctor whose acquaintance I had made on the boat, who also found themselves unable to reach their original destinations, left for Bitol the next day.

Arrived at Bitol, I at once made inquiries about the next step farther, and found that Prilip, about twenty-five miles farther on, was still in the hands of the Serbians, though its evacuation was expected any minute, and even now the road from Bitol to Prilip was not considered safe on account of marauding Bulgarian *comitadjes*, or irregulars. However, the English Consul had to go out there, and he said he would take us with him to see how the land lay, and whether we were needed in the hospital there.

I spent the afternoon prowling round Bitol, mostly in the Turkish quarter.

The next day we went with the Consul to Prilip—though up to the last moment I was afraid we should not go, as there was so much talk about the road not being safe—some of us in the touring car and the rest in a motor-lorry, with an escort of Serbian soldiers, all armed to the teeth. I took my camp bed and blankets with me, on the off chance of being able to stay at Prilip, as I was gradually edging my way up to the Front, leaving the rest of my baggage in Bitol to be sent after me. We got there without any mishap, keeping a sharp look-out for Bulgarian patrols. We found a Serbian military hospital at Prilip, and I asked the *Upravnik* or Director if I might stay and work there, to which he consented, but added that he was afraid that it would not be for long, as they were expecting to have to fly before the Bulgarians any day. I accordingly got a room at the hotel, and the Consul left me an orderly to look after me, named Joe, who could speak a little English. I was very pleased at getting into a Serbian hospital again in spite of all difficulties, as the opinion in Salonica seemed to be that it was impossible; but I must say I felt rather lost when the cars went back that evening and I was left alone, the only Englishwoman in Prilip.

The first thing I did was to turn all the furniture, including the bed, out of the room in the tenth-rate pub, which was the best hotel that Prilip boasted, and made Joe scrub the floor and put in my own camp bed.

I take the following extract out of my diary, written on my first night in Prilip:

Monday, 8th, 8.30 p.m.—I am sitting up in bed in my sleeping sack, writing this in a very small room in S—— Hotel, Prilip. The room contains (besides my camp bed) a rickety chair, and a small table with my little rubber basin, a cracked mirror and my faithful tea-basket. From the cafe below comes a deafening chorus of Serbian soldiers. I am glad there is a good lock on the door, as someone is making a violent effort to come in, and from the fierce altercation going on between him and the boy-chambermaid, scraps of which I can understand, he is apparently under the impression that I have taken his room—I may have for all I know, but anyhow the proprietor gave it to me.

The view from my window is not calculated to inspire confidence either. It looks on to a stableyard full of pigs, donkeys and the most villainous-looking Turks squatting about at their supper. These, I tell myself, are the ones who will come in and cut my throat if Prilip is taken tonight, as I don't think any responsible person in the town knows I am here. However, if I live through the night things will probably look more cheery in the morning.

In the middle of the night I was awakened by another fearful racket in the passage. "That's done it," I thought, sitting up in bed with my electric torch in one hand and my service revolver in the other, "it's like my rotten luck that the Bulgars should pitch on tonight to come in and sack the town." However, a very few minutes convinced me that it was only two drunks coming up to bed, and, telling myself not to be more of a fool than nature intended, I turned over and went to sleep again.

I think my morbid reflections must have been brought on by the supper I had had. Joe, my orderly, had, for reasons best known to himself, taken me to a different restaurant to the one where we had been to lunch with the consul, assuring me that it was much better; it was not, very much worse, in fact, though I should not have thought such a thing could be possible. It was full of soldiers and *comitadjes* drinking. At first I could get no food at all, and when it did come it was uneatable. I had supper with an American doctor I met in the town next night, and he informed me that food was so scarce and dear in Prilip that to get anything of a meal you had to have your meat in one restaurant, your potatoes in another, and your coffee in a third!

Next morning I went round to the hospital, and in the afternoon one of the doctors took me round and introduced me to the Serbian chief of police, who was most friendly and polite, got me a nice little room close to the hospital, and apologised for not being able to ask me to come to his house as his guest as his wife was ill. This is the sort of courtesy that has always been extended to me in Serbia; they think the best of everything they can offer is not too good for the stranger within their gates, and I began to feel much cheered up.

There were not very many wounded in the hospital, but a great many sick, and dysentery cases beginning to come in rapidly. I was soon quite at home there, being used to the ways of Serbian hospitals. The director was going to Bitol for a few days, and I asked him to ask the head of the Sanitary Department there, Dr. Nikotitch, if I might join a regimental ambulance as nurse, as I heard that the ambulance of the Second Regiment was some miles farther up the road, just behind the Front. The Second and Fourteenth Regiments were then holding the Baboona Pass, a very strongly fortified position in the mountains, against the Bulgarians.

I stayed about a week in the hospital; there was plenty of work to do—in fact, to have done it properly there would have been enough for a dozen nurses, as dysentery was rapidly becoming an epidemic, and the hospital was soon full up; we could take in no more. We were fearfully short of everything, beds, bedding, drugs, and we simply had to do the best we could with practically no kind of hospital appliances. Any kind of proper nursing was impossible, most of the patients lying on the floor in their muddy, trench-stained uniforms.

One afternoon two of the doctors motored out to the ambulance of the Second Regiment and took me with them. We stopped first at the ambulance of the Fourteenth, where we found twenty unfortunate dysentery cases lying on the bare ground in two ragged tents groaning. We had a long chat with the doctor of the Second Regimental ambulance, and had coffee and cigarettes in his room—a loft over the stable. That is to say, I did not do much of the talking as he was a Greek, and besides his own language only talked Turkish and not very fluent Serbian, although later on, strange to say, when I joined the same ambulance, we used to carry on long conversations together in a kind of mongrel lingo very largely helped out by signs.

We visited a large empty barracks on our way back, and made arrangements for it to be turned into a dysentery hospital, as this disease was beginning to assume serious proportions, and our hospital was full up. This was never carried out, however, owing to the Bulgarians' rapid advance a few days later.

The next day the director came back, and brought with him papers whereby I was officially attached to the ambulance of the Second Regiment; and it was part of my extraordinary luck to have just hit on this particular regiment, which is acknowledged to be the finest in the Serbian Army. Everybody was extremely kind to me in the hospital, and all the doctors asked me to stay there and work, saying I could have no idea of the hardships of ambulance life; but as I knew that it would not be many days before we all had to clear out of Prilip before the advancing Bulgarians, and that would mean my going back to Salonica, and losing all chance of staying with the Serbians (whom I had grown thoroughly attached to in my work among them for the last year and a half), I adhered to my resolution to throw in my lot with the army.

I always had my meals at the hospital now, and we had quite a merry supper that night, and they all drank my health, declaring they would see me back in three days, when I had been frozen out of my small tent on the hills, where it was already bitterly cold. The next afternoon I went all round the hospital and said goodbye to everyone; I was very sorry to leave my patients, they are so affectionate, and always so grateful for anything one does for them. One young soldier was my special pet; he had been driven mad from the shock of a shell bursting close to him, though he was not wounded. He was such a nice gentle lad, and I used to spend a good bit of time with him, coaxing him to swallow spoonfuls of milk, as he would not take anything from anyone else, though the Bolnichars—hospital orderlies—were very kind to him. I heard afterwards that he lived till the hospital was evacuated, but died at Bitol. A good many of the men were from the Second Regiment, and when they heard I was going to their ambulance we only

FRENCH STEAMER WITH BOATS SLUNG OUT READY AND ESCORT

AMBULANCE OF SECOND REGIMENT. OX WAGGONS WHICH HAVE JUST
BROUGHT IN WOUNDED

said *au revoir*. They assured me we should meet again when they were sent back to their regiment, as they would come and see me directly they had the smallest pain.

It was rather late in the day when Joe and I finally set out in a very rickety carriage commandeered by martial law, with a very unwilling driver, and a horse that could hardly crawl. The harness, which was tied up with bits of string, kept coming to pieces, and the driver kept stopping to repair it. Joe began to look very uneasy, and kept peering round in the gathering dusk for any signs of wandering Bulgarian patrols, or *comitadjes*, as it was a very lonely road. At last, after what seemed an interminable time, we arrived at the ambulance, which was on the grass by the side of the road. They were not expecting me then as it was late, and the Serbians turn in soon after sunset. There was apparently nowhere to sleep and nothing to eat. One of them took us round to the doctor's quarters, the same loft I had visited a few days before, not far from the ambulance. He turned out full of apologies, and said that he had had notice that I was coming that day, but that as it was so late he had given me up.

It seemed a bit of a problem where I was to sleep, but eventually some of the soldiers turned out of one of their small bivouac tents. These tents are only a sort of little lean-to's, which you crawl into, just the height of a rifle, two of which can be used instead of poles. You seem a bit cramped at first, but after I had lived in one for a couple of months I did not notice it. All the tents were bunched up together, touching each other, with four soldiers, or hospital orderlies, in each. I insisted, to their great surprise, in having mine moved to a clean spot about fifteen yards away from the others, and some more or less clean hay put in to lie upon. There was a good deal of excitement and confusion, the whole camp turning out and assisting. They could not imagine why I wanted it moved, and declared that the Bulgarian *comitadjes* would come down in the night and cut my throat before the sentry knew they were there.

Afterwards, when I was more used to war, and accustomed to sleeping in the middle of a regiment, and to sleeping when and where one could, in any amount of noise, I used to laugh at my scruples then, and only wondered they were all as good-tempered and patient as they were with what must have seemed to them my extraordinary English ideas. The doctor sent me down some supper of bread and cheese and eggs, and presently came down himself and sat on the grass beside me as I ate it, and altogether they all did their best to make me comfy, and were as amiable as only Serbians can be when you rouse them out in the middle of the night and turn everything upside down. It reminded me somewhat of my arrival in Valjevo, at the beginning of the typhus epidemic, when owing to the vagaries of the Serbian trains I was landed at the hospital at 3 a.m., after everyone had given me up. After I had finished my supper I crawled into my tent, tightly rolled myself up into the blankets as it was a very cold night, and slept like a top on my bed of hay.

CHAPTER 2

We Start to Retreat

Next morning we all turned out at daybreak, and I got a better view of my surroundings. The ambulance itself consisted of one largish tent, where the patients lie on their clothes on very muddy straw, until they can be removed to the base hospital by bullock-wagon. This is done as often as transport permits. There were a few cases of dressings, drugs, etc., in the tent, and a small table for writing at. There were about twenty patients in at one time, some of them sick and some wounded. About a dozen little tents, similar to mine, for the soldiers and ambulance men, and two or three wagons completed the outfit.

There was a Serbian girl, about seventeen, helping; she was very unlike any other Serbian woman I had ever met, lived and dressed just like the soldiers, and was very good to the sick men. She spoke German very well, so that we understood each other and became very good friends; she gave me lots of tips, and though I had been under the impression that I knew something about camping out and roughing it, having done so already in various parts of the world, she could walk rings round me in that respect. The first thing the men did after I had had some tea with them by the camp fire was to set to work to convince me of the error of my ways, and to move my little tent back to its old spot before any harm could happen to me. We don't have breakfast in Serbia, but have an early glass of tea, very hot and sweet, without milk.

The doctor came down shortly afterwards to prescribe for the men who were sick, and then a couple of orderlies and myself dressed the wounded ones, those who were able to walk coming out of the tent and squatting down on the grass outside, where there was more room, and light enough to see what you were doing. They kept straggling in all day from Baboona, where there was a battle going on; it was not far away, and the guns sounded very plain. There were not very many seriously wounded, but I am afraid that was because the path down the mountains is so steep that it is almost impossible to get a badly wounded man down on a stretcher. Any who are able to walk down do so, and they were glad to get their wounds dressed and be able to lie down. At lunch-time we knocked off for a couple of hours, and I went back with the doctor to his loft. We had lunch in great style, sitting on his bed, there being no chairs, and with a blue pocket-handkerchief spread out between us for a tablecloth. He said they were expecting to have a retreat at any moment, and that we must always be in readiness for it as soon as the order arrived.

All the patients we had were to go off that afternoon if the bullock-wagons arrived. This question of transport is always a terrible problem; in many cases bullock-wagons are the only things that will stand the rough tracks, although here there was a good road all the way to Bi-tol, and had we had a service of motorcars we could have saved the poor fellows an immense amount of suffering. Imagine yourself with a shattered leg lying in company with three or four others on the floor of a springless bullock-wagon, jolting like that over the rough roads for twenty or thirty miles. When I was in Kragujewatz we used to get in big batches of wounded who had travelled like that for three or four days straight from the Front, with only the first rough dressing which each man carries in his pocket.

The wagons came that afternoon, but only two or three for the lying-down patients; several poor chaps who were so sick they could hardly crawl had to turn out and start on a weary walk of a good many miles to the nearest hospital at Prilip. One man protested that he would never do it, and I really didn't think he could, and said so; how-ever, the ambulance men, who were well up to their work, explained that it was absolutely imperative that all should get off into safety day by day, otherwise when the order came suddenly to retreat we might find ourselves landed with an overflowing tentful of sick and wounded men, and no transport available on the spot. "Go, brother," they said kindly, "*Idi polako, polako*" ("Go slowly, slowly"), and fortified with a drink of cognac from the ambulance stores, and a handful of cigarettes from me, he and the others like him set off.

We all turned in prepared that evening, and I was cautioned to take not even my boots off. Later on, sleeping in one's clothes didn't strike me as anything unusual; in fact, two months later, when we had finished marching and arrived at Durazzo, it was some time before I remembered that it was usual to undress when you went to bed, and that once upon a time, long, long ago, I used to do the same. In the middle of the night a special messenger arrived with a carriage from the English Consul at Bitol, advising me to come back at once, and that a motorcar would meet me in Prilip, and take me back to Bitol. I knew perfectly well that I should not be able to find the motorcar in the middle of the night in Prilip, which is as dark as the nethermost regions, there not being a lamp in the town, and that it would probably mean sitting up in the carriage in one of those dirty little streets all night; so I said all right, I would see about it in the morning, and went to bed again. In the morning I had another look at the telegram, and as it was not an order to go back, but only advising me strongly to do so, I said I meant to stop. They all seemed very pleased because I said I wanted to stick with the Serbians, and, as we all sat round the camp fire in the bitter cold of a November sunrise, we drank the healths of England and Serbia together in tin mugs full of strong, hot tea.

Later on during the day came another telegram, and I must say that the English Consul at Bitol was a perfect trump in the way he did his duty by stray English subjects and looked after their safety, before he finally had himself to leave for Salonica. A Serbian officer was sent out from somewhere, and he said that if I liked to throw in my lot with them and stop he would send out a wagon and horses, in which I could live and sleep, and in which I could carry my luggage. I hadn't very much of the latter, and what I had I was perfectly willing to abandon if it was any bother, but he wouldn't hear of that; and in due course the wagon arrived, and proved, when a little hay had been put on the floor to sleep on, a most snug abode.

The next day the wounded kept straggling in all day, faster than we could evacuate them, and when the order came at ten o'clock that night that the regiment was forced to retreat from Baboona, and that the ambulance was to start at once, we had sixteen wounded in the tent, twelve of them unable to walk. The Serbian ambulances travel very light, and half an hour after receiving our orders we were on the move, the men being adepts at packing up tents and starting at a moment's notice. At the last moment, while the big ambulance tent was being taken down, a man with a very bad shrapnel wound in the ankle was carried in, and as it was blowing a gale, and we couldn't keep a lamp alight, I dressed it by the light of a pocket electric torch, which I fortunately had with me. They said at first that he would have to go on as he was, but as I knew very well that it might be three or four days before he would get another dressing I insisted on them getting out some iodine, gauze, etc., and kneeling in the mud, and with some difficulty under the circumstances as the tent was being taken down over my head, I cut off his boot and bloody bandages (he had been wounded in the morning) and cleaned and dressed the wound. He was awfully good, poor fellow, though it hurt him horribly, and he hardly made a murmur. Then two ambulance men carried him out to the ox-wagon, three of which had appeared from somewhere, I don't know where.

I found the Kid, as I called her, had been working like a Trojan in the pitch dark and pelting rain helping the men through the thick, slippery mud down the bank to the road, and had settled four men, lying down, in each wagon, that being all they could hold, and had also decided the knotty point which should be the four unlucky ones who had to walk—these four being, I may say, quite well enough to walk, but naturally not being anxious to do so. When they were all started off, she and I clambered into our wagon, and the whole cavalcade set off in the pitch dark, not having the faintest idea (at least, we had not, I don't know if anybody else had) where we were going to travel to or how long for. We were a long cavalcade with all the ambulance staff, the *komorra* or transport, and a good many soldiers all armed, and a most unpleasant night we had rumbling along in the dark, halting every few miles, not knowing whether the Bulgars had got there first and cut the road in front of us, or what was happening. It was bitterly cold besides, and as the Kid and I were black and blue from jolting about on the floor of our wagon I began to wonder how the poor wounded ever survived it at all.

A little way on we picked up a young recruit who said he was wounded and couldn't walk; our driver demurred, saying that he had had orders that no one else was to use our wagon, but we said, of course, the poor boy was to come in if he was wounded. He lay on my feet all night, which didn't add to my comfort, though it kept them warm. He was evidently starving, so we gave him half a loaf of bread that we had with us, and some brandy out of my water-bottle, and he went to sleep.

Putting brandy in my water-bottle had been suggested to me by a tale a young Austrian officer, a prisoner, who was one of my patients in Kragujewatz hospital, told me. Poor boy, he had been badly wounded in the leg, and was telling me some of his experiences during the war and about the terrible journey after he was wounded, travelling in a bullock cart. He said he had a flask full of brandy, and that was a help while it lasted. When that was all gone he filled up the flask with tea, which was pretty good, too, as it had a stray flavour of brandy still, and then when he had drunk all that he put water in, and that had the flavour of tea!

The next morning our "wounded hero "hopped off quite unhurt, and we couldn't help laughing at the way we had been done. It was a bitterly cold dawn, and we found to our sorrow that the recruit had not put the cork back in my water-bottle, and the rest of the brandy had upset, as had also a bottle of raspberry syrup which the Kid set great store by. I once upset a pot of gooseberry jam in a small motor-car, and it permeated everything until I had to take the car to a garage to be washed, and go and take a bath myself before I could get rid of it; but it was not a patch in the way of stickiness to a pot of raspberry syrup let loose in a jolting wagon, and we were very glad to get out at daybreak, after eight hours' travelling, to walk a bit to stretch our legs, and also to wipe off some of the stickiness with some grass.

We came through Prilip that night, and were rather doubtful how we should get through, but though the people standing about glowered at us, and we heard a few shots in the distance, nothing much happened, and only one man got slightly hurt.

We arrived somewhere between Prilip and Bitol at sunrise, and made a big fire and waited for further orders when the colonel of the regiment should arrive. Presently he rode up with his staff, and I was introduced to Colonel Militch, the commandant of the Second Regiment. My first impression of him was that he was a real sport, and later on, when I got to know him very well and had the privilege of being a soldier in his regiment, I found out that not only was he a sport, but one of the bravest soldiers and most chivalrous gentlemen anyone ever served under. We stood round the fire for some time and had a great *powwow*; my Serbian was still in an embryo stage, but the colonel spoke German.

We were all very cold and hungry, but one of the officers of the staff, who was a person of resource, made some rather queerish coffee in a big tin mug on the fire, and we all had some, and it tasted jolly good and hot, and then the colonel produced a bottle of liqueur from a little handbag, and we drank each other's healths. I got to know that little handbag well later—it used always to miraculously appear when everybody was cold, tired and dying for a drink.

After a couple of hours the ambulance went on about a mile and pitched camp, and I went with them. The Kid went to sleep in the wagon and I did the same outside on the grass. The doctor sent me a piece of bread and cheese, which I casually ate on the spot, not liking to wake the Kid up, but afterwards I was filled with remorse for my thoughtlessness, when I was convicted by her later on for not being a good comrade at all, as it appeared it was the only eatable thing in camp; but, as I was new and green at "retreating," at that time it never dawned on me: I learnt better ways later on. I made her some tea with my tea-basket, but it was not very satisfying.

Later on in the day the commandant of the Bitol Division, Colonel Wasitch, and an English officer came up in a car. I was introduced to them, and went with them in the car somewhere up the road to visit a camp. The commandant of the division went off to attend to business, leaving the English officer and myself to amuse ourselves as we liked.

Here we were witnesses of a case of corporal punishment. I relate it because some people think this is quite a common occurrence; it is not, cruelty is absolutely foreign to their natures. Some people once talked of setting up a branch of the "Prevention of Cruelty to Animals" in Serbia, and were asked in astonishment what work they supposed they would find to do; who ever heard of a Serbian being cruel to child or animal? Corporal punishment, that is to say, a certain number of strokes with a stick (maximum 25—schoolboys will know on what part), is the legitimate and recognised way of punishing in the Serbian Army, and the sentence is carried out by a non-commissioned officer. As an officer once explained to me, some punishment you must have in the interests of discipline, and what else *can* you do in wartime, when you are on the move every day? Particularly was it so at this most critical juncture, when it would have been fatal for the whole army had the men been allowed to get out of hand.

This question of corporal punishment in the Serbian Army has so frequently been brought up to me by English and French officers that I purposely mention it, as I have always tried to thoroughly disabuse their minds of any idea that the men were indiscriminately knocked about. I may add that it is not so very many years since flogging was abolished in our own navy, and no doubt in course of time the Serbian Army will follow suit. The most popular officer I knew, who was absolutely adored by his own men, was extremely ready to award corporal punishment. "My soldiers have got to be *soldiers*," he replied curtly to me once, and his men certainly were. These things always depend largely on the particular officer, of course. I think the Serbian soldier, more than anyone else I have ever come across, can excel as a "passive resister" when he is under an unpopular officer; while all the time keeping himself just within the bounds of discipline, he will contrive to avoid doing anything he does not wish to do, while he is extraordinarily "clannish" and loyal to one whom he likes. In the critical moments in a battle it is not the question whether an officer is "active" or "reserve" that counts, or whether he has passed through his military academy or risen from the ranks, but whether the men will follow him or not.

Captain —— and I walked back to the ambulance together and found that some of the orderlies had got a pig from somewhere and were roasting it with a long pole through it over the camp fire: it smelt jolly good, and as we were very hungry, having had nothing to eat but a piece of bread and cheese, we accepted their invitation to have supper with them with alacrity. As soon as it was cooked we all sat round the big fire in a semicircle, and ate roast pig with our fingers, there being no plates or cutlery available, and Captain —— said he had never tasted anything so good in his life, and wished he could come and join our ambulance altogether.

At some of the other fires dotted about they were roasting some unwary geese which had been foolish enough to stray round our camp. As the inhabitants of the houses had fled leaving them behind we certainly could not call it looting. Looting was very firmly checked; the Serbian is far from being the undisciplined soldier in that respect that some people suppose.

CHAPTER 3

A Ride to Kalabac and a Battle in the Snow

It snowed hard in the night and most of the next day and was bitterly cold, blowing a gale, but my wagon was a good bit snugger than the tent. The colonel and his staff had quarters in a loft over a little cafe just along the road, and after lunch the commander of the division, who came with two English officers, took the Kid and me with them in their cars some miles back along the road towards Prilip, where we all walked about and inspected the new positions part of the regiment was to take up. The Kid went back to Bitol in the ear with them that evening to fetch some clothes, and I never saw her again, though I believe she did want to come back to us later on.

I used to sit over the camp fires in the evenings with the soldiers, and we used to exchange cigarettes and discuss the war by the hour. I was picking up a few more words of Serbian every day, and they used to take endless trouble to make me understand, though our conversations were very largely made up of signs, but I understood what they meant if I couldn't always understand what they said. It was heart-breaking the way they used to ask me every evening, "Did I think the English were coming to help them?" and "Would they send cannon?" The Bulgarians had big guns, and we had nothing but some little old cannon about ten years old, which were really only what the *comitadjes* used to use. If we had had a few big guns we could have held the Baboona Pass practically for any length of time, for it was an almost impregnable position.

I used to cheer them up as best I could, and said I was sure that some guns would come, and that even if they did not they must not think that the English had deserted them, as I supposed they had big

166

plans in their head that we knew nothing about, and that though we might have to retreat now everything would come right in the end. It was touching the faith they had in the English, whom they all described as going "*slowly but surely.*" They were very much excited when they saw the two English officers, as they were sure they had come to say some English troops were coming.

One day, however, one thousand new English rifles did come, and there was great rejoicing thereat.

With the courtesy which always distinguishes the Serbian peasant, they used always to stand up and make room for me, and bring a box for me to sit on in the most comfortable place by the fire, out of the smoke, and I used to spend hours like this with them. Under happier circumstances they would all have been singing their national songs and dancing, but, though there were many fine singers among them, nothing would induce them to sing: they were too broken-hearted at being driven back. One man did start a song one night to please me, but he broke down in the middle and said he knew I would understand why he could not sing.

There was deep snow on the ground, and it was bitterly cold, and the men used to anxiously ask me if I managed to keep warm at night, as they huddled up together, four in one tiny tent, for warmth, and seemed to rather fear that they might find me frozen to death some morning in my wagon, but I was really quite warm enough.

The next day, while we were doing the dressings, a man came in who had walked from Nish, twenty-two days' tramp. He was a cheery soul, and said he felt very fit, but he looked as thin as a rake. We all crowded round him to hear the news. He said that the town of Nish was evacuated and everyone gone to Krushavatz.

Commandant Militch told me he was sending for his second horse, so that I could ride her. When she arrived she proved to be a very fine white half-Arab, who could gallop like the wind, and I grew very fond of her. She had a passion for sugar, and always expected a bit when she saw me. The *commandant* had moved his quarters a few miles farther up the road towards Prilip to a small deserted *hahn*, or inn, consisting of two small rooms by the roadside. It was close to the village of Topolchar. I had been cautioned not to stray away from the camp by myself, as it was very unsafe; only a few days before Bulgarian *comitadjes* had swooped down and taken prisoner a Serbian soldier who had gone to fetch some water not a quarter of a mile from his own camp. One bright sunny morning, however, the hills looked so tempting that

ROASTING THE PIG

AN AMBULANCE FIELD STATION

I went for a stroll and wandered on farther than I intended. I was out of sight of the camp, when suddenly I heard voices behind some trees, though I could not see anybody, and I knew that none of our men were camping near. Discretion conquering curiosity, I beat a dignified retreat at a brisk walk, as I was quite unarmed at the time, and they told me when I got back it was a good thing I did. I took no more constitutionals over the hills while in that neighbourhood, anyhow, for I had no wish to cut off my career with the army by suddenly disappearing, as no one would know what had become of me.

One day I rode over on Diana, my white mare, to see the *commandant* and his staff at the *hahn*. They all welcomed me most warmly, inviting me to stop to supper, sleep there, and ride out next day with them to the mountain of Kalabac, to visit the positions there. I accepted joyfully. They said I could either sleep there near the stove or have my wagon brought up, if I was not afraid of being too cold. I decided in favour of the wagon, as the *hahn* was already pretty crowded; so they telephoned for it, and in due course it arrived with my orderly. It was a grey-covered wagon, and I had christened it "My little grey home in the west." A house on wheels is an ideal arrangement, as if you take it into your head to sleep anywhere else you go off and your house simply follows you. It was planted exactly opposite the door, with a sentry to guard me.

The *commandant*, in spite of all his troubles, was full of fun, and even in the darkest and most anxious hours in the tragic weeks that followed kept up everyone's spirits and thought of everyone's comfort before his own. After a most hilarious supper I turned in, as we were to make an early start next morning.

Next day the *commandant*, his adjutant and I, with four armed *gendarmes*, rode off to Kalabac. It was a lovely day, and we had about two hours' ride across country to the first line of trenches. The *commandant* and I used to have a race whenever we got to a good bit of ground. He was a fine rider, and, as the horses were pretty well matched, we used to get up a break-neck speed sometimes, and had some splendid gallops. About a year before in Kragujewatz I was riding with a Serbian soldier who had been sent with a horse for me, and he said: "What did I want to be a nurse for?" and tried to persuade me not to go back to the hospital, but to join the army then and there, regardless of my poor patients expecting me back.

The first line of trenches that we came to were little shallow trenches dotted about on the hillside, with about a dozen men in each. We sat in one of them and drank coffee, and I thought then that I should be able to tell them at home that I had been in a real Serbian trench, little thinking at the time that I was going to do it in good earnest later on under different circumstances.

After that we went on up to another position right at the top of Kalabac. It was a tremendous ride, and I could never have believed that horses could have climbed such steep places, or have kept their feet on some of the obstacles we went over, but these horses were trained to it, and could get through or over anything. Just the last bit of the way we all had to dismount, and, leaving the horses with the *gendarmes*, did the rest on foot. There was no need for trenches there, as it was very rocky, and there was plenty of natural cover. Major B—— and another officer met us near the top, and he and the *commandant* went off to discuss things. It happened to be Captain Pesio's "*Slava*" day. This "*Slava*" day is an institution peculiar only to the Serbians, and which they always keep most faithfully.

Every family and every regiment has one. It is the day of their particular patron saint, and is handed down from father to son. It is kept up for three days with as much jollification as circumstances permit, even in wartime. I have been the guest at plenty of other *Slava* days in Serbia, but I never enjoyed anything so much as I did that one. We sat round the fire on boxes or logs of wood under the shelter of a big overhanging rock, with a most gorgeous panorama of the country stretching for miles round, and had a very festive lunch, and all drank Captain Pesio's health. In the middle of lunch I had my first sight of the enemy, a Bulgarian patrol in the distance, and orders were promptly given to some of our men to go down and head them off. The men all seemed to be in high spirits up there, in spite of the cold, and some of them were roasting a pig, although I suppose that was a "*Slava*" luxury for them, not to be had every day.

It was evening by the time we left, and we slipped and slid down the mountain again by moonlight. When we got back to the first trenches which we had visited we made a short halt, and sat in an officer's little tent and drank tea. He had certainly not been at war for four years without learning how to make himself comfortable under adverse circumstances, and had brought it down to a fine art. He had a tiny little tent, one side of which was pitched against a bank, and in the bank there was a hole, with a large fire in it, and a sort of tunnel leading up to the outer air for a chimney. His blanket was spread on some boughs woven together for a bed, and he was as snug and warm as a toast when he did get a chance to sleep in his tent, which was apparently not very often. He was very popular with everyone, and the *commandant* spoke particularly of his bravery. We were quite sorry to leave and turn out into the cold night air.

We had a long ride home, ending up with a hard gallop along the last bit of road, and it was late when we got back to the *hahn*. There was a big fire going in the iron stove, and we soon thawed out. The *commandant* sat down at his table and dictated endless despatches to his adjutant, while I dosed on his camp bed till about ten, when he finished his work for the time being and we had supper. Every now and then there would be a rap at the door, and an exhausted, half-frozen rider would come in bearing a despatch from one of the outlying positions on the hills.

I was very sorry afterwards that I had not taken my camera with me up to the positions, but I was not sure at the time if they would like me to, though afterwards they told me I might take it anywhere I liked.

There was another small ambulance here in charge of the proper regimental doctor, and in the afternoon everyone was ordered to move up into the village, Topolchor, and find rooms there. The soldiers were all delighted at the prospect of getting under a roof of any kind, though I felt quite sorry at leaving my Little Grey Home. The doctor got me a nice big empty room in what was formerly the school. There was a pile of desks and tables filling up one side of it, and a stove, but otherwise no furniture. After my orderly had unpacked my camp bed and lit the stove I had some visitors: three or four old native women, who came up and inspected me and all my belongings closely, and seemed deeply impressed with the extraordinary luxury in which an Englishwoman lived, with a room to herself, a bed *and* a rubber bath! I had been making futile efforts, by the way, for the last few days to make use of this same bath, in spite of my orderly's repeated assurances that you could not have a bath in wartime, which I found afterwards to be strictly true. I did not succeed even here, owing to the lack of water and anything to carry it in.

The villagers themselves, those who had not already fled in terror, seemed to live in the most abject poverty, huddled together in houses no better than pigsties. The place was infested by enormous mongrel dogs, which used to pursue me in gangs, barking and growling, but they had a wholesome respect for a stone, and never came to close quarters.

Next morning I went for a long ride with the *commandant* to inspect some more of the positions. He had to hold an enormous front with only two regiments, and, as we were outnumbered by the Bulgarians by more than four to one, when the latter could not break through our lines they simply made an encircling movement and walked round them, and, as there were absolutely no reserves, every available man being already in the fighting line, troops had to abandon some other position in order to cut across and bar their route. Thus we were constantly being edged back, and were very many times in great danger of being surrounded.

We were fighting a rear-guard action practically all the time for the next six weeks—a mere handful of troops, worn out by weeks of incessant fighting, hungry, sick, and with no big guns to back them up, retreating slowly and in good order before overwhelming forces of an enemy who was fresh, well equipped and with heavy artillery. It was no use throwing men's lives away by holding on to positions when no purpose could be gained by it, though the colonel felt it keenly that the finest regiment in the army should have to abandon position after position, although contesting every inch, without having a chance of going on the offensive. It was heartbreaking work for all concerned, and the way they accomplished it is an everlasting credit to officers and men alike.

My orderly told me he had heard we were going that evening, so he packed up everything, camp bed included, and put it in my wagon. We hung about all the evening expecting to get the order to go at any moment, as the horses were always kept ready saddled in the stable, and you simply had to "stand by" and wait until you were told to go, and then be ready to get straight off. Eventually, however, the *commandant* came back and said we were not going that night, and we had a quiet supper about ten o'clock and turned in, with a warning to be up early in the morning. As my bed was packed up I rolled myself up in a blanket on the floor, and my orderly did likewise at the other side of the stove and kept the fire up. It was snowing hard and frightfully cold.

At daybreak we did move, but not very far, only to the little *hahn* by the roadside; and there we stood about in the snow and listened to a battle which was apparently going on quite close; although we strained our eyes we could see nothing—there was such a frightful blizzard. A company of reinforcements passed us and floundered off through the deep snow drifts across the fields in the direction of the firing. There was no artillery fire (I suppose they could not haul the guns through the snow), but the crackle of the rifles got nearer and nearer, and at last about midday they were so close that we could hear the wild *"Hourrah, Hourrahs"* of the Bulgarians as they took our trenches, and as the blizzard had stopped for a bit we could see them coming streaking across the snow towards us, our little handful of men retreating and reforming as they went. The Bulgarians always give the most blood-curdling yells when they charge. The ambulance was already gone, and there were only the colonel and his staff, myself and the doctor left. The horses were brought out, and the order came to go, but only about three miles to where the big ambulance was camped with whom I had been at first.

There was a river between the *hahn* and this ambulance, and the road went over a bridge. This bridge was heavily mined and was to be blown up as soon as our men were over, thus cutting off, or anyhow considerably delaying, the Bulgarians, as the river was now a swollen icy torrent. We sat round the fire of the ambulance and dried our feet. Some of the men were soaking to the knees, having no boots, but only *opankis*, leather sandals fastened on with a strap which winds round the leg up to the knee. Later on some wounded were brought in, given a very hurried dressing, and despatched at once to the base hospital. The majority of them seemed to be hit in the right arm or wrist, but I am afraid perhaps the worst wounded never reached us. One poor fellow who was hit in the abdomen was, I am afraid, done for; he would hardly live till he got to the hospital.

We heard no more firing till late in the afternoon, when all at once it broke out again quite close, and with big guns as well this time. We wondered how on earth they had been able to get them across the river, but the explanation was forthcoming when we heard that the bridge, although it had ten mines in it, had failed to blow up—the mines would not explode; no one knew why. I floundered through the snow up a little hill with some of the others to see if we could see anything, but we could not see much through the winter twilight except the flashes from the guns momentarily lighting up the snow banks, and hear the noise of the shells as they whistled overhead.

This had been going on for a couple of hours now, and the Greek doctor was getting into a regular funk because they had had no orders to move, though it was all right as we had no wounded in the tent to be carried away, and no one else was worrying about it; but he finally sent a messenger up to the *commandant*, as he seemed to think the ambulance had been forgotten. A couple of days afterwards the men told me with much scorn that that afternoon had been too much for him, and that he did a retreat on his own and never came back to the ambulance again. I was just thinking of looking round for something to eat, as I had had neither breakfast nor lunch, and had been much too busy to think about it, when the order arrived for the ambulance to pack up and move, and the tents came down like lightning.

The soldiers were all retreating across the snow, and I never saw such a depressing sight. The grey November twilight, the endless white expanse of snow, lit up every moment by the flashes of the guns, and the long column of men trailing away into the dusk wailing a sort of dismal dirge—I don't know what it was they were singing—something between a song and a sob, it sounded like the cry of a Banshee. I have never heard it before or since, but it was a most heartbreaking sound.

My *saïs* (groom) brought Diana round to me. I asked him if he had been told to do so, and he said "No," but that I "had better go now." He shook his head dubiously, murmuring, "Safer to go now," when I told him I was coming later on with the *commandant* and his staff.

War always seems to turn out exactly the opposite to what you imagine is going to happen. Such a great proportion of it consists of "*an everlastin' waiting on an everlastin' road*," as someone has already written. Bairnsfather hits it off exactly in his picture of the young officer with his new sword: how he pictures himself using it, charging at the head of his company, and how he really does use it, toasting bread over the campfire! I had some wild visions in my head—as I knew the *commandant* would wait until the last moment—of a tremendous gallop over the snow, hotly pursued by Bulgarian cavalry. I imagine I must once have seen something like it on a cinematograph.

What, however, really did happen was that, having received permission to stop, I sat for four hours in company with seven or eight officers who were waiting for orders, on a hard bench in a freezing cold shed, which in its palmier days might have been a cowhouse. I was ravenously hungry, and sucked a few Horlick's milk tablets I found in my pocket, but they did not seem so satisfying as the advertisements would lead one to suppose. However, presently the jolly little captain, whose tent I described on Kalabac, came in, followed by his soldier servant bearing a hot roast chicken wrapped up in a piece of paper! Where in the world he got it I can't think. We had no knives or forks, but we sat side by side, and each took hold of a leg and pulled till something gave. It tasted delicious! He shared it round with everybody, and I don't think had much left for himself. Although he came straight from the trenches, where he had been fighting incessantly and had not slept for three nights himself, he was full of spirits and livened us all up, and we little thought that it was the last time we were to see him. I was terribly sorry to hear a few days later of the tragic death of my gay little friend.

The firing had ceased, as it usually does at night, and at last, about nine o'clock, the *commandant* appeared and the horses were brought out, and instead of the wild cinema gallop I had pictured we had one of the slowest, coldest rides you can imagine. There was a piercing blizzard blowing across the snowy waste, blinding our eyes and filling our ears with snow; our hands were numbed, and our feet so cold and wet we could hardly feel the stirrups. We proceeded in dead silence, no one feeling disposed to talk, and slowly threaded our way through crowds of soldiers tramping along, with bent heads, as silently as phantoms, the sound of their feet muffled by the snow.

I pitied the poor fellows from the bottom of my heart—they were so much colder and wearier even than I was myself, and I wondered where the "glory" of war came in. It was exactly like a nightmare, from which one might presently wake up. My dreams of home fires and hot muffins were brought to an abrupt termination by the *commandant* suddenly breaking into a trot, when I found my knees were "set fast" with the cold, and I had a very painful five minutes till they loosened up. After a long time we turned off the road across some snowy fields. I followed close behind the *commandant*, who always made a bee line straight ahead through everything; and after our horses had slipped and scrambled through a hedge, a couple of deep ditches and a stream we eventually got to the village of Mogilee, I think it was called.

The soldiers bivouacked in some farm outhouses, and we were received by some officers in a big loft. They had a huge stove going and supper ready for us. We finished up the long day quite cheerily, even having a bottle of champagne that a *comitadje* brought as a present to the *commandant*. We all slept that night in the loft on the floor, I being given the place of honour on a wide bench near the stove, while the other six or seven selected whichever particular board on the floor took their fancy most, and spread their blankets on it. Turning in was a simple matter, as you only have to take off your boots; and, though the atmosphere got a bit thick, we all slept like tops.

175

THE TENT I SLEPT IN FOR TWO MONTHS

SERBIAN ARMY TRUDGING ALONG

CHAPTER 4

A Cold Night Ride

We were all up at daybreak next morning as usual; no good Serbian sleeps after the first streak of light. It was still snowing fearfully hard, making it impossible to go out, though the *commandant* and his staff captain rode out somewhere all the morning. We had sundry cups of tea and coffee during the morning and a pretty substantial snack of bread and eggs and cold pig about ten. I protested that I was not hungry, and that we should have lunch when the *commandant* came in, but they reminded me of what had happened to me yesterday in the matter of meals, and might possibly happen again tomorrow, and advised me to eat and sleep whenever I got a chance. They were old soldiers and spoke from experience, and I subsequently found it to be very good advice.

It was a long day, as we had nothing to do. In the afternoon the doctor started to teach me some Serbian verbs, and afterwards we all played "Fox and Goose," and I initiated them into the mysteries of "drawing a pig with your eyes shut," and any other games we could think of with pencil and paper to while away the time.

About dusk we set forth again to a small village, Orizir, close to Bitol. It was pitch dark as we splashed across a field and a couple of streams to another little house which we occupied. It consisted of two tiny rooms, up a sort of ladder, with a fair-sized balcony in front. The balcony was quite sheltered with a big pile of straw at one end, and I elected to sleep there, though they were fearfully worried about it, and declared I should die of cold, in spite of my protestations that English people always sleep much better in the open air than in a hot room with all the windows shut. Foreigners always look upon English people as more than half mad on the subject of fresh air, especially at night.

The next day my orderly, who was in a great state of mind, and seemed to think that I would lose caste with his fellow orderlies if I persisted in sleeping on the balcony, told me that he had found another room for me in a *hahn* by the roadside, where I accordingly slept the next night, and subsequently we all moved down there. I actually got my long-sought-for bath that day, my resourceful man borrowing a sort of stable for me for an hour and fixing it up for me. As all old campaigners know, a certain kind of live stock, and plenty of them, is the inevitable accompaniment to this sort of life, and is one of its greatest trials, though you do get more or less used even to that. I burnt a hole, in my vest cremating some of them, but judging by the look of my bathroom, where the soldiers had been sleeping, I am not at all sure that I did not carry more away with me than I got rid of.

While I was engaged in this interesting occupation my orderly called out that the English Consul was there and wished to see me, so I hastily dressed and went out to interview him. He had come in a car to take me back to Salonica with him if I wanted to go, which of course I did not; so he just drove me into town to pick up a large case of cigarettes which I had previously ordered from Salonica for myself and the soldiers and anyone else who ran short of them, and he also gave me a case of tins of jam and one of warm woollen helmets, which were very much appreciated by the men. He said he thought I was quite right to stop, and we parted warm friends.

When I got back I found the staff captain, who was the *commandant's* right hand, just going out for another cold ride. He had had fever for the last two or three days, and looked so fearfully ill that I begged him not to go, as, however much he might, and did, boss everybody when he was well, he might let himself be looked after a little bit when he was ill. Rather to my surprise he submitted quite meekly, and let me dose him with quinine, and tuck him up in his blankets by the stove, and as he was shivering violently I told his orderly to make him some hot tea and stand outside the door to see that no one came in to disturb him. As the tea did not seem to be forthcoming, I went out presently to see what was up, and found him with several of his fellow orderlies sitting in the snow round the camp fire having a meal of some kind. He said he had made the tea, but had not any sugar; so I asked some of the others.

"Now, don't you say '*Néma*' to me," I said, before he had time to speak, "but go and find some, because I know perfectly well you have got it." It is a Serbian peculiarity, which I had found out long ago, that

178

whenever you first ask for a thing they invariably say "*Néma*" ("There isn't any"). I have frequently been told that in a shop with the thing lying there under my eyes, because the man was too lazy to get up and get it. They thought it a great joke, and of course produced it, and "Don't say '*Néma*' to me "became a sort of laughing byword amongst some of the men afterwards whenever I asked for anything. They have a keen sense of humour, and are always ready for a laugh and a joke, and their gaiety and high spirits bubble up even under the most adverse circumstances.

The rest of the staff and I then made a fire in the other little room, and sat there and played chess and auction bridge, and were making a terrific noise over the latter, when the *commandant* came back. If you really want an amusing occupation, likely to give rise to any amount of discussion and argument, try teaching auction bridge to three men who have never seen it played before, in a language your knowledge of which is so slight that you can only ask for the simplest things in the fewest possible words. You'll find the result is a very queer and original game.

The next afternoon, it having at last stopped snowing, I walked over to visit my old friends in the ambulance a couple of miles up the road, and we sat by the camp fire and pored over the map of Albania, whither we should soon be going, and discussed the war as usual. When I got back about sunset I found the *commandant* had gone to visit a company who were camped about a mile and a half up the road, and his adjutant was waiting for me, as we thought it would be a good opportunity to give away some of the warm woollen helmets while it was so cold. Accordingly, followed by a couple of men carrying the wool helmets, some cigarettes and a few pots of jam, we started for the camp. It turned out to be the Fourth Company of the First Battalion, strange to say, the very company that I afterwards joined, though I didn't guess that at the time. It was a most picturesque scene with the little tents all crowded together, and dozens of big camp fires blazing in the snow with soldiers sitting round them; they all seemed very cheery in spite of the bitter cold.

We had a great reception, the whole company was lined up, and under the direction of their company commander I gave every seventh man a white woollen helmet—unfortunately there were not enough for each man to have one—and every man a couple of cigarettes, and my orderly followed with half a dozen large pots of jam and a spoon, the men opening their mouths like young starlings waiting to be fed.

179

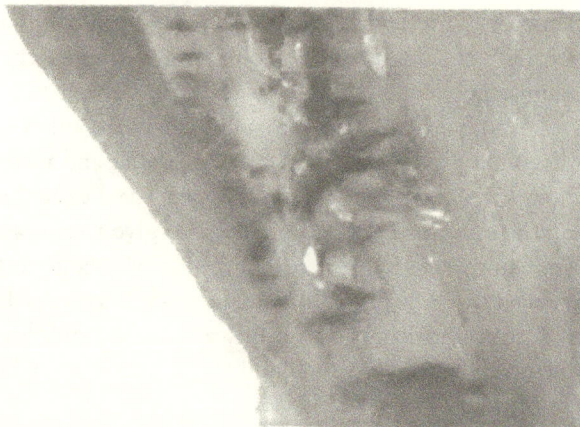

An early start packing up

Reinforcements in the snow

This is a national custom in Serbia; directly you visit a house your hostess brings in a tray with a pot of jam, glasses of water and a dish with spoons on it. You eat a spoonful of jam, take a drink of water, and put your spoon down on another dish provided for that purpose. It is very amusing to see a stranger the first time this is presented to him; he generally does not know what he is supposed to do, or whether he is to dip the jam into the water, or *vice versa*, and how many spoonfuls it would be polite to eat, Serbian jam being extraordinarily good. One Englishman I knew wanted to go on eating several spoonfuls, and I had gently but firmly to check him.

I was introduced to all the officers, and a great many of the men who were pointed out to me as having done something very special. One of the men was wearing an English medal for "distinguished conduct in the field." The men seemed awfully pleased with their little presents; they never have anything in the way of luxury—no jam, sweets or tobacco served out to them with their rations, no parcels or letters from home (at this time), no concerts or amusements got up for their benefit, none of the things that our Tommies hardly regard in the light of luxuries, but necessities. No one who has not lived with them can imagine how simply they live, how much they think of a very little, and what a small thing it takes to please them. After that little ceremony was over we sat round the officers' camp fire and a young sergeant—a student artist—played the flute very well indeed, and they sang some of their national songs. It was all so friendly and fascinating that we were very loath indeed to tear ourselves away, and I promised to come back next day and take their photographs, but next day they were not there, having been ordered off at dawn to hold some positions up on the hills.

Among other sundry oddments in my luggage I had a box of chessmen and a board, and as several of them could play we whiled away many weary hours when we had nothing else to do playing chess. The *commandant* and I were very evenly matched, and we used to have some tremendous battles, sometimes long after everyone else was asleep, and always kept a careful record of who won. Some of the others were very keen on it too, and those who were not playing would stand round and offer advice. I used sometimes to think, as I listened to the sounds of hurried packing up going on all round while we sat calmly playing chess, that the Bulgars would walk in one day and capture the lot of us, chessboard and all.

About 9 p.m. next night the *commandant* gave the order to start, and we walked the first mile, the horses being led behind, I suppose to get used to the roads, which were one slippery sheet of ice. When we got to Bitol, which was quite close, we went to the headquarters of the *commandant* of the division, and sat there till about midnight, while he and our *commandant* discussed matters. We met Dr. Nikotitch there again, and he and Commandant Wasitch asked me if I really had made up my mind to go on. They said the journey through Albania would be very terrible, that nothing we had gone through so far was anything approaching it, and that they would send me down to Salonica if I liked.

I was not quite sure whether having a woman with them might not be more of an anxiety and nuisance to them than anything else, though they knew I did not mind roughing it; and I asked them, if so, to tell me quite frankly, and I would go down to Salonica that night. They were awfully nice, though, and said that "for them it would be better if I stopped, because it would encourage the soldiers, who already all knew me, and to whose simple minds I represented, so to speak, the whole of England." The only thought that buoyed them up at that time, and still does, was that England would never forsake them. So that settled the matter, as I should have been awfully sorry if I had had to go back, and I believe the fact that I went through with them did perhaps sometimes help to encourage the soldiers.

We left there soon after midnight, and rode all night and most of the next day. The *commandant* and his staff captain drove in a wagon, the same one that the Kid and I had driven in on the first night of the retreat. They asked me whether I would rather come in the wagon with them or ride, as the roads were simply terrible, but I elected to ride and chance Diana going on her head, which she did not do, however, as the *commandant*, with his usual thoughtfulness, had had her roughed for me a few days before. We rode very, very slowly, always through crowds of soldiers, pack-horses and donkeys, halting about every hour at little camp fires along the roadside made by our front guard, where we sat and warmed our feet for about a quarter of an hour till the tired soldiers could catch us up, there being frequent halts for them to rest for a few minutes. I rode alongside the adjutant and another officer, and was very glad that my orderly had filled my thermos flask with hot tea, with a good dash of cognac in it, which the three of us consumed while riding along.

The roads were really fearful, one solid sheet of ice, and the adjutant's horse came down so often that eventually he had to walk and lead it. Occasionally we all used to get down and walk for a bit to warm our feet, which became like blocks of ice, but the going was so hard that we were glad to mount again. I say "mount," but in reality, what between wearing a heavy fur coat and getting colder and stiffer and wearier, it was more a sort of crawl up Diana's side that I did; fortunately she was a patient animal, and used to stand still. It soothed my feelings to see that I was not the only one, several of the others having nearly as much difficulty in mounting. They were all so friendly, and I had more than one "Good luck to you" shouted after me. It was not really such a hard ride as we had expected, though, as stopping at the little camp fires and chatting with the men round them made a nice break.

About daybreak we arrived at a *hahn*, where we found the ambulance again, and the *commandant* and the captain got their horses there, and we all walked, and later on rode, up and up a winding road, up a mountain. It was bitterly cold, and every few yards we passed horrible looking corpses of bullocks, donkeys and ponies, with the hides and some of the flesh stripped from them; sometimes there were packs, ammunition and rifles thrown away by the roadside, but very, very few of the latter; a soldier is very far gone indeed before he will part with that. Of course everywhere swarmed with spies, and we stopped a man and a boy in civilian clothes carrying baskets; they protested that they were going down to do some marketing or something of that sort, but whatever it was they wanted to do they were told they could not do it, and gently but firmly turned back.

At the very top we stopped at the ruins of a filthy little hut, where a halt was called and the field telephone rigged up. We built a fire outside—it was too dirty to go inside—under the wall, and had some coffee, and tried, very unsuccessfully, to get out of the howling, bitter wind. The soldiers sat about and rested, and we stayed there until late in the afternoon. We were to spend the night at Resan, some way down the other side, and about 3 o'clock the doctor said he was going down there, and I might as well come down with him and look for a room. Wily young man, he was petrified with cold himself and didn't like to say so, so had previously told the staff captain that *I* was cold and wanted to go into the town, and that, as I could not go by myself, hadn't he better escort me? He let this out afterwards, and I was very indignant with him, but he was quite unabashed. He used to love teasing me, calling me "Napoleon" because I rode a white horse, and we were constantly sparring.

My orderly, after a long search, found me quite a decent little room in a house close to the Caserne, where the staff were to be quartered. The family consisted of two old ladies and a girl, who all fell on my neck and hugged me, rather to my embarrassment. One of the old ladies explained volubly that she had once had something—I never could quite make out whether it was a husband or a cat—and had lost it, and I was now to take its place in the family circle.

We all sat round the stove in my little room, which seemed quite a luxurious palace to me now, and I made them real English tea with my little tea-basket, and the poor old things seemed quite enchanted, as they had neither tea nor sugar in the house, and they fussed over me, and could not do enough for me.

The next morning I stayed in bed till nearly eight, and, after dressing leisurely, went up to see the *commandant* and staff, who said they had begun to think they had lost me. About five o'clock my orderly came in in a great state of excitement and wrath, declaring that he did not know what to do with my things as the wagon had been taken for something else, and that the *commandant* and staff were all gone. He was an excitable person, and used to get these panics occasionally, and, as I knew perfectly well that whatever happened they would not leave me behind, I told him not to be such an ass, but to go and get my horse and I would go and find out for myself, as I could not get any sense out of him.

I happened to meet the *commandant* in the street, and, as I fully expected, we had supper quietly, and did not stir till 9 p.m. We nearly always did ride at night. We left very quietly, and walked the first bit of the way through the mud, and then rode up a beautiful serpentine road, which had originally been made by the Turks, through what looked as if it might be beautiful country if you could only see it. All the way along there were soldiers and camp fires, which looked so pretty twinkling all over the hills through the fir trees, and we made frequent halts while the *commandant* gave his orders.

I thought we were going to ride all night, and it was a pleasant surprise when we turned off the road, and put our horses at a steep muddy bit of mound at the top of which was an old block-house, one of the many built by the Turks and dotted all over that part of the country. The telephone was rigged up there, and it was full of officers and soldiers; the ground all round was a perfect sea of mud, and there were soldiers everywhere. I had not the faintest idea whether we were going to stop there half an hour or for the rest of the night, and I don't suppose anybody else had either, except, perhaps, the *commandant*. I sat by the stove for some time, and finally lay down on the floor on some straw that looked not quite so dirty as the rest, though that is not saying much, but when I woke up some hours later I got the impression that I had strayed into a new version of the Black Hole of Calcutta. The whole floor was absolutely covered so thickly with sleeping men that you could not put your feet down without treading on them. I counted up to twenty-nine and then gave it up because I saw several more come in afterwards, though where they managed to wedge themselves in I do not know. The *commandant* had left the telephone and was sleeping peacefully among the others; the only person awake was a very big, good-looking *gendarme*, who was keeping the stove stoked up, although it was already suffocatingly hot.

The Serbians laugh at me because I declare that they always pick their *gendarmes* for their good looks; they are certainly a magnificent set of men. This one inquired if I wanted anything, as soon as he saw that I was awake, and I asked him if he would fetch me my thermos flask full of tea, which he would find in Diana's saddle-bag. He had never seen a thermos flask before, and when he brought it back and I shared the tea with him he was perfectly thunderstruck to find it still hot. He couldn't make it out at all, and seemed to think that in some extraordinary way Diana must have had something to do with it, and I shouldn't be surprised if next day he put a bottle of tea in his own saddle-bag to see if his horse would be equally clever.

About 5 a.m., while it was still dark, I woke up again so boiling hot that I could not stand it any longer, and crawled out cautiously over the sleeping men, treading on a good many, I am afraid, though they did not seem to object, and took a walk round; but, as it was raining and the mud appalling, I did not stay outside long. There was one camp fire still going, and what I took to be a large bundle covered over with a sack beside it. Here's luck, I thought, something to sit on beside the fire, and down I plumped, but got up again quickly when it gave a protesting grunt and a heave, and I found I had sat down on a man. After that I sat on a tin can in the cold passage for some time and waited for daybreak.

CHAPTER 5

We Say Goodbye to Serbia and Take to the Albanian Mountains

The next morning we rode on and camped at another blockhouse. The field telephone was going all the time here, and evidently the news was anything but satisfactory. I did so heartily wish that I knew more Serbian and could understand more of what was going on. I was so keenly interested in what was happening and where the various companies were and how they were getting on, and it was maddening when breathless despatch riders used to come in from the trenches, and I could only gather a little bit of what they were saying, and generally miss the vital point. The *commandant* and his staff captain used to pore over maps at the table, and, although they would not have minded my knowing anything, of course I could not bother them with questions. Sometimes if Commandant Militch was not busy he used to show me the various positions on the map, and tell me where he was moving the men to. It was such a frightfully anxious time for him, he had to hold the threads of everything in his hands; everything depended on him, the lives and safety of all the men, and despatch riders and telephone calls gave him very little rest.

On this particular occasion we made an unusually sudden start, and he explained to me afterwards, as we were riding along, that the Bulgarians had made another of their encircling movements, and got round our position, and very nearly cut the road in front of us, and there was considerable probability at one moment that we might have to take to the mountains on foot, to escape being taken prisoners. However, he was able to send some troops round, and they succeeded in getting down in time to cut them off. Being taken prisoner by the wild Bulgarians would have been no joke.

We halted in the afternoon in a field where a company was resting, some of the Third Call. There are three calls. First, Second and Third—the young men, middle-aged and the old fellows, who as a general rule are only used for light work, guarding bridges, railways, etc., but now had to march and do the same as the young men, and it came very hard on them.

The Serbians live hard and seem to age much quicker than our men do, as they call a man of forty or forty-five an old man, and they look it, too. The peasants usually marry very young, about twenty; and as we sat and chatted round the fires several of this Third Call told me their ages and how many sons they had serving in the army. We camped that night in a house in the village, the usual room up a flight of wooden steps. These houses never seem to have any ground floor. I suppose in these disturbed parts the inhabitants find it safer to live at the top of a ladder.

The next day the snow had all cleared away, and, strange to say, it was like a lovely spring morning. While I was drinking a cup of coffee out on the verandah a young soldier came up and wanted to see the *commandant*. He looked fearfully thin and ill, and told me that he and ten others had had nothing to eat for eleven days. I was horror-struck, and asked the staff captain if such a thing could be possible, but what he literally meant was that they had been stationed somewhere where they had received no regular rations, and had had to live by their wits or on what the people in the village would give them. Be that as it may, there was no mistaking the fact that he looked very hungry, and I gave him a large piece of bread and cheese which I had in reserve and some cigarettes. He put the piece of bread and cheese in his pocket, and when I asked him why he did not eat it then and there said he was going to take it back and share it with the others! To see real unselfishness one must live through bad times like these with men, when everyone shares whatever he has.

We rode on into a filthy, muddy little village, where we spent the afternoon. I went for a walk up the hill, through a company of soldiers who were resting on the grass, belonging to some other regiment whom I did not know, and coming back I was stopped and closely questioned by an officer. He did not know who I was, and was evidently considerably puzzled. He wanted to know where I had been and why, and seemed to think that I might have been paying a visit to the Bulgarians, who were close on our heels as usual. He looked rather incredulous when I said that I had only been for a walk, and I

A COLD HALTING PLACE

THE BLOCKHOUSE WHERE WE ALL SLEPT

thought he was going to arrest me on the spot pending further investigations, until I pointed to the brass letter "2" on my shoulders, and said I was with the Second Regiment, and that the commandant was down in the village. Then he let me pass. The *commandant* had taken the regimental numbers off his own epaulettes when I first joined and fastened them on the shoulders of his new recruit, and I was very proud of them. The *commandant* was very much amused when I told him about it, and told me not to go and get shot in mistake for a spy.

In the evening we rode on by Ockrida Lake, on and on along the most awful roads, with mud up to our horses' knees, till we finally came to a building and camped in the loft.

Next morning I rode out with the *commandant* to inspect the positions. There was a battle going on a little way away in the hills, and we could hear the guns plainly and see the shrapnel bursting. There was a lovely view of the lake, and on the other side you looked away towards the black Albanian hills, and we thought as we looked towards them that this was the very last scrap of Serbia, and that we should soon be driven out of it. Coming back we passed a company by the roadside, and the *commandant* stopped and talked to them, and anyone could see how popular he was, and how pleased they always were to see him. He made them a long speech, cheering them up and telling them to stand fast now and not despair, as some day we would all march back into Serbia together.

We rode to Struga, on the Ockrida Lake, that night, and went up to the headquarters of the *commandant* of the division, where we found him and his whole staff in bed. The room seemed absolutely full up with camp beds and sleeping men, but they got up with great cheerfulness, put on their boots and brushed their moustaches and entertained us with tea and coffee till about 1 a.m., when we repaired to an empty hotel, where there was plenty of room for all, for a few hours' sleep.

We were routed out long before dawn, and after a cup of Turkish coffee in the kitchen all turned out into the main street of the village of Struga. In the bitterly cold grey dawn we stood around in black, churned-up mud, shivering, hungry, and miserable. The discouraged soldiers trailed along the road, in the half-light of a winter morning, and altogether we looked the most hopelessly forlorn army imaginable, setting our faces towards the dark, hard-looking range of snow-capped mountains which separate their beloved Serbia from Albania. It was the last town in Serbia, and we were being driven out of it into exile. It made me feel sad enough, and what must it have been to them, for they are so passionately attached to their own country that they never want to leave it, and the Serbian peasant feels lost and homesick ten miles from his own native village.

A great deal has been written about the physical sufferings of the soldiers at this time; hunger and pain they can stand, but this home sickness and despair, the feeling that they were friendless, an army in exile, not knowing what had become of all their loved ones in Serbia, this was what really broke their hearts and took the spirit out of them far more than their other sufferings. They looked upon me almost as one of themselves, and officers and men alike used to tell me about their homes until I felt almost as if it was my own country that had been invaded, and that we were being driven out of. "I am leaving my youth behind me in Albania," said one young officer to me as we sat looking away into the stormy Albanian sunset one evening. How many of us before we won through to the coast were to leave not only our youth but our health and some of us our lives on those Albanian mountains!

Very glad I was that morning to see the sun rise and things brighten and warm up a little. We rode to a Turkish village up on a hill overlooking Struga and the lake, and from there we watched the bridge burn which connected the Turkish quarter of the town with the part held by our soldiers, thus delaying the Bulgarian pursuit, but not for long. We stayed there two or three days with fighting going on all around. The Bulgarians kept up a heavy bombardment with their big guns over the Struga road, responded to by our little antiquated cannon. We looked right down on it, and watched the shrapnel bursting all day and the enemy gradually coming closer.

Some of our artillery was concealed in a little wood just below the village, and presently the enemy got the range of this beautifully, and the shells were falling fast among the trees. The doctor had been down there, and he brought me back a piece of shell which had fallen right into the middle of the men's kitchen and upset all their soup, scattering them in all directions, but, wonderful to say, not hurting anybody, and he had promised to take me with him next time. I was sitting on the wall with the staff captain watching it and wanted very much to go down, but he said I had better not. "Do you mean only I 'had better not,' or that I 'am not to'?" I enquired meekly, having a wholesome respect for military discipline by now.

"No," he said positively, "I mean you are not to." So there was nothing more to do but to salute and say "*Rasumem*" ("I understand"), the Serbian reply to an order. I thought it rather hard, however, to be chipped afterwards by the officer in command down there for not coming down to help them and I could not persuade him that I had done my best.

The Turkish inhabitants of the village were very friendly, and the old man who owned our house used to bring us large presents of walnuts. They did not seem to like the Bulgarians at all, and explained to us by signs that the Bulgarians were bad people and very cruel and would cut their throats if they came into the village. The villagers used to sit about all day watching the shrapnel. They seemed very pleased to see us, and several of the children used to bring me presents of nuts and flowers. They used to look at me with great curiosity, and could not quite make out who or what I was. I found a couple of miserable looking Austrian prisoners who were wandering round the village, who were too ill to go away with the others and had been left behind.

We left there a few days afterwards at three o'clock in the morning and rode down to a valley where the Fourteenth Regiment were camped, and spent the rest of the night sitting round their camp fire. We looked so funny in the early morning light all squatting round the fire, the commandant included, toasting bits of cheese on the ends of pointed sticks; it tasted extremely good washed down by some of the *commandant's* "Widow's Cruse" of liqueur. I wanted to take a photograph of us, but the light wasn't good enough. Afterwards I curled up by the fire with the soldiers and went to sleep, and the sun was shining brightly when I woke to find the whole regiment sitting up with their shirts off busily hunting the "first hundred thousand," and I wished I could do the same myself. "Shirts off" always seemed by unanimous consent to be the order of the day directly there was a halt for any length of time, and I should think there must have been very large "catches" sometimes.

We crossed the frontier through Albania that afternoon, and went along a winding road up a hill till right at the top you looked down on beautiful Lake Ockrida and Serbia on one hand and on the other barren Albania. Here we halted for a few minutes, and sort of said goodbye to Serbia, and then rode on in silence into the Albanian valley, where we camped at a sentry's little hut on a hillock.

The next day the *commandant* took me with him for his usual ride up into the positions. The hills were very rough and steep, but our plucky horses managed it all right. We stopped at one Albanian village, on the way which was invested by some of our troops. These Albanian villages were a perfect picture of squalor and filth. I don't know what the people subsist on, but they seem to live like animals. I had always pictured the Albanian peasants as a very fine picturesque race of men wearing spotless native costume, and slung about with fascinating looking daggers and curious weapons of all kinds, but the great majority of those I saw, more especially in the small towns, were a very degenerate looking race indeed.

We had intended going up to some positions which the Fourteenth Regiment were holding, and where a battle was then in progress, but before we got up there we got word that they had had to retreat, and saw them coming back down the mountain side; so we had to stop where the field telephone was rigged up, and the *commandant* was very busy for a long time giving orders, etc. He was away for some time, and I lay down and went to sleep on the grass. With their usual charming manners a couple of soldiers came up, telling me they had a fire over there, and one of them fetched his blanket and spread it by the fire for me to lie on, while the other one rolled up his overcoat for a pillow.

The Serbian peasant's manners are not an acquired thing, depending upon whether they have been well or badly brought up, but seem to be natural and part of themselves, and as such are always to be depended upon. People who do not know anything about them have sometimes asked me if I was not afraid to go about among what they imagine to be a race of wild savages, but quite the opposite is the case. I cannot imagine anything more unlikely than to be insulted by a Serbian soldier. I should feel safer walking through any town or village in Serbia at any hour of the night than I should in most English or Continental towns.

Coming back in the dark, Diana fell on to her head in a ditch, and I rolled off out of the way, as I did not want her to lie down on top of me, but I got unmercifully chipped for "falling off." I was tired, and had besides a splitting headache; so I went and lay down in my tent when we got in. My orderly came and tucked me up, made me some tea, and told the men near not to make a noise, and altogether made up for any shortcomings he might have by being exceedingly sympathetic. I had not intended going in to supper, but he was so persuasive about it, telling me there was, as he expressed it, such a "fine supper," and was so anxious for me to have some, that I finally went in. About

9.30 p.m. we packed up again and rode for a couple of hours to another little house, where we found some officers, who turned out of their beds—which they invited us to sit on while they entertained us with tea—after which the *commandant*, captain, adjutant and myself turned in thankfully, not for very long, as we had to start at 3 a.m. the next morning.

We rode till daylight, and then camped on a hill near the ambulance. There was no house here, so the staff borrowed one of the ambulance tents, and I pitched my little one alongside of it. The Second Regiment were camped on the same hillside, and the next morning the commander of the First Battalion, Captain Stoyadinovitch, came in to see the colonel before going with his battalion to take up the positions. I asked if I might go with him, and he said I might; so I rode off with him at the head of the battalion, little thinking how long it would be before I saw the commandant and his staff again, and that was how I came afterwards to be attached properly to a company, and became an ordinary soldier.

CHAPTER 6

Fighting on Mount Chukus

We rode all that morning, and as the commander of the battalion, Captain Stoyadinovitch, did not speak anything but Serbian, nor did any other of the officers or men, it looked as if I should I soon pick it up. The staff had also shifted their quarters at the same time, and while we were riding up a very steep hill where Captain S—— had to go for orders Diana's saddle slipped round, and by the time some of the soldiers had fixed it again for me I found he had got his orders and disappeared. I asked some of the soldiers which way he had gone, and they pointed across some fields; so I went after him as fast as Diana could gallop. I met three officers that I knew, also running in the same direction, and all the men seemed to be going the same way too. The officers hesitated about letting me come, and said, "Certainly not on Diana," who was white and would make an easy mark for the enemy; so I jumped off and threw my reins to a soldier.

"Well, can you run fast?" they said.

"What, away from the Bulgars!" I exclaimed in surprise.

"No, towards them."

"Yes, of course I can."

"Well, come on then," and off we went for a regular steeplechase, down one side of a steep hill, splashing and scrambling through a torrent at the bottom of it and up another one equally steep, a sturdy lieutenant leading us over all obstacles, at a pace which left even all of them gasping, and I was thankful that I was wearing riding breeches and not skirts, which would have certainly been a handicap through the bushes. I wondered how fast we could go if occasion should arise that we ever had to run away *from* the Bulgarians, if we went at that pace *towards* them. Though no one had breath to tell me where we were going, it was plain enough, as we could hear the firing more clearly every moment. We finally came to anchor in a ruined Albanian hut in the middle of a bare plateau on the top of a hill, where we found the commander of the battalion there before us, he having ridden another way. The Fourth Company, whom we had already met once that morning, were holding some natural trenches a short way farther on, and we were not allowed to go any farther. The Bulgarians seemed to have got their artillery fairly close, and the shrapnel was bursting pretty thickly all round. We sat under the shelter of the wall and watched it, though, as it was the only building standing up all by itself, it seemed to make a pretty good mark, supposing they discovered we were there, which they did very shortly.

An ancient old crone, an Albanian woman, barefooted and in rags, was wandering about among the ruins, and she looked such a poor old thing that I gave her a few coppers. She called down what I took at the time to be blessings on my head, but which afterwards I had reason to suppose were curses. The shells were beginning to fall pretty thickly in our neighbourhood, and our battalion commander finally said it was time to move on. He proved to be right, as three minutes after we left it the wall under which we were sitting was blown to atoms by a shell. My old crone had disappeared in the meantime to a couple of wooden houses on the edge of the wood. We had to cross a piece of open ground, which we did in single file, to reach this wood, and before we got to it we got a whole fusillade of bullets whistling round our ears from the friends and relations of the old lady upon whom I had expended my misplaced sympathy and coppers. These were the sort of tricks the Albanians were constantly playing on us from the windows of houses, whenever they got a chance.

We got down through the wood to where we left our horses, waited for the Fourth Company to join us, which they presently did, and then rode on, halting for a time, not far from where some of our artillery were shelling the enemy down below in the valley. The officer in charge showed me how to fire off one of the guns when he gave the word, and let me take the place of the man who had been doing it as long as we stayed there.

It was dark when we got to our camping ground that night, close to where the colonel and his staff were settled, so I sent for my blankets and tent, which I had left with them, and camped with the battalion. After a light supper of bowls of soup we sat in a circle round the camp fire till late, smoking and chatting. The whole battalion was camped there, including the Fourth Company, with whom I had previously spent an evening at their camp in the snow, and I thought it very jolly being with them again. It did not seem quite so jolly, however, the next morning, when we were aroused at 3 a.m. in pitch dark and pouring rain, everything extremely cold and horribly wet, to climb into soaking saddles, without any breakfast, and ride off goodness knows where to take up some new position.

It was so thick that we could literally not see our horses' ears; I kept as close as I could behind Captain S——, and he called out every now and again to know if I was still there. We jostled our way through crowds of soldiers, all going in the same direction up a steep path turned into a mountain torrent from the rain, with a precipitous rock on the near side, which I was told to keep close to, as there was a precipice on the other. A figure wrapped up in a waterproof cloak loomed up beside me in the darkness and proved to be the commander of the Fourth Company. He presented me with firstly a pull from his flask of cognac, which was very grateful and comforting, and secondly a pair of warm woollen gloves, which he had in reserve, as my hands were wet and frozen.

This young man had a most useful faculty of having a "reserve" of everything one could possibly want, which he always produced just at the right moment, when one did want it. He had not done four years' incessant campaigning without learning everything there was to know about it, and prided himself upon always having a "reserve," from a tin of sardines or a piece of chocolate when you were hungry and had nothing to eat, to a spare bridle when someone's broke, as mine did one day, although he seemed to carry no more luggage than anyone else. We rode like this till after daylight, and then sat on the wet grass under some trees and had a plate of beans; they tasted very good then, but I've eaten them so often since that now I simply can't look a bean in the face. They asked me if I was going to tackle the mountain on foot with them, or if I would rather stay there with the transport.

I went with them, of course. Mount Chukus is 1,790 metres high from where we were then, and it certainly was a stiff climb. We left our horses there—I had been riding a rough mountain pony of Captain S——'s—and the whole battalion started up on foot. There was no path most of the way, and in places it was so steep that we had to scramble along and pull ourselves up by the bushes, over the rocks and boulders, and in spite of the cold and wet we were all dripping with perspiration. We of necessity went very slowly, making frequent halts to recover our breath and let the end men catch up, as we did not want to lose any stragglers. It must be remembered that not one of these men but had at least one old wound received either in this or some previous war, and a great number had five or six, and this climb was calculated to catch anybody in their weak spot.

We arrived at the top about 4 p.m., steady travelling since 3 a.m. that morning, most of which had been uphill and hard going. One officer with an old wound through his chest, and another bullet still in his side, just dropped on his face when we got to the top, though he had not uttered a word of complaint before.

At the very tip-top we camped amongst some pine trees and put up our tents; it was still raining hard and continued to do so all that night, and everything was soaking—there didn't seem to be a dry spot anywhere. The little bivouac tents are made in four pieces, and each man carries one piece, which he wraps round him like a waterproof when he has to march in the rain; and, if it is not convenient to put up tents, rolls himself up in it at night. We made fires, though we were nearly blinded by the smoke from the wet wood; someone produced some bread and cheese and shared it round, and then we all turned in. It was so cold and wet that I crawled out again about 2 a.m., and finished the night by the fire, as did three or four more uneasy souls who were too cold to sleep. My feet were soaking, so I stuck them near the fire and then went to sleep, pulling my coat over my head to keep off the rain, and it was not until some time afterwards that I discovered that I had burnt the soles nearly off my boots.

I felt hearty sympathy for a soldier I heard one day in Durazzo being reprimanded by an officer for having half his overcoat burnt away—"Do you think you were the only one who was cold? Why didn't *that* man and *that* man burn their clothes? they were just as cold," and I thought guiltily of my own burnt boots. Later on the next day the sun put in an appearance, as did also the Bulgarians. The other side of the mountain was very steep, and our position dominated a flat wooded sort of plateau below, where the enemy were. One of our sentries, who was posted behind a rock, reported the first sight of them, and I went up to see where they were, with two of the officers. I could not see them plainly at first, but they could evidently see our three heads very plainly.

The companies were quickly posted in their various positions, and I made my way over to the Fourth, which was in the first line; we did not need any trenches, as there were heaps of rocks for cover, and we laid behind them firing by volley. I had only a revolver and no rifle of my own at that time, but one of my comrades was quite satisfied to lend me his and curl himself up and smoke. We all talked in whispers, as if we were stalking rabbits, though I could not see that it mattered much if the Bulgarians did hear us, as they knew exactly where we were, as the bullets that came singing round one's head directly one stood up proved, but they did not seem awfully good shots. It is a funny thing about rifle fire, that a person's instinct always seems to be to hunch up his shoulders or turn up his coat collar when he is walking about, as if it were rain, though the bullet you hear whistle past your ears is not the one that is going to hit you. I have seen heaps of men do this who have been through dozens of battles and are not afraid of any mortal thing.

We lay there and fired at them all that day, and I took a lot of photographs which I wanted very much to turn out well; but, alas! During the journey through Albania the films, together with nearly all the others that I took, got wet and spoilt. The firing died down at dark, and we left the firing line and made innumerable camp fires and sat round them. Lieut. Jovitch, the commander, took me into his company, and I was enrolled on its books, and he seemed to think I might be made a corporal pretty soon if I behaved myself. We were 221 in the Fourth, and were the largest, and, we flattered ourselves, the smartest, company of the smartest regiment, the first to be ready in marching order in the mornings, and the quickest to have our tents properly pitched and our camp fires going at night. Our company commander was a hustler, very proud of his men, and they were devoted to him and would do anything for him, and well they might. He was a martinet for discipline, but the comfort of his men was always his first consideration; they came to him for everything, and he would have given anyone the coat off his back if they had wanted it. A good commander makes a good company, and he could make a dead man get up and follow him.

That evening was very different to the previous one. Lieut. Jovitch had a roaring fire of pine logs built in a little hollow, just below what had been our firing line, and he and I and the other two officers of the company sat round it and had our supper of bread and beans, and after that we spread our blankets on spruce boughs round the fire and rolled up in them. It was a most glorious moonlight night, with the ground covered with white hoar frost, and it looked perfectly lovely with all the camp fires twinkling every few yards over the hillside among the pine trees. I lay on my back looking up at the stars, and, when one of them asked me what I was thinking about, I told him that when I was old and decrepit and done for, and had to stay in a house and not go about any more, I should remember my first night with the Fourth Company on the top of Mount Chukus.

The next morning our blankets were all covered with frost and the air was nippy, but got warmer as the sun got up, and one soon gets used to the cold when one is always out of doors.

We took up our positions again behind the same line of rocks soon after sunrise. In the afternoon the firing got very hot, and the Bulgars got a sort of cross fire on, so that the bullets were also spitting across the plateau where we had our fire last night, and they seemed to be getting up nearer round another ridge. Our cannon were posted somewhere below on our left commanding the road, and we could watch how things were going on between them and the Bulgarian artillery by the puffs of white smoke. We had a few casualties, but not so very many.

We stayed there all day till dark, and it got very cold towards sunset, kneeling or lying on our tummies; sometimes we just sniped as we liked, and sometimes fired by volley as the platoon sergeant gave the order, "*Né shanni palli*" ("Take aim, fire"). I had luckily always been used to a rifle, so could do it with the others all right.

One drawback to Chukus was that there was very little to eat and no water, or at least hardly any, it having to be fetched in water-bottles from a long distance, or melted down from the snow which still hung about there in deep drifts. We used to fill billy-cans with snow and melt it over the fire. The men had long ago finished their ration of bread which they carried in their knapsacks and only had corn cobs, which they roasted over the camp fires; we had also almost rim out of cigarettes and tobacco.

About 9 p.m. the order came to retire; coming up the mountain was bad enough, but going down was worse. It was lucky there was a moon. We went down a different side along a path covered with thick slippery mud and very steep, and, as I had no nails in my boots and not much soles, I found it hard to keep my feet. Halfway down we met another battalion, and I was delighted to meet my old friend whose "*Slava* day" we had celebrated on the top of Mount Kalabac, and who wanted to know what in the world I was doing here. We found the horses at the bottom, and then the men marched, and I and those of the officers who had horses rode all night through a long defile in the mountains. It was a very narrow track, with a mountain up one side and a precipice on the other which effectually prevented one from giving way to the temptation to go to sleep while riding.

We picked up the rest of the regiment soon after daybreak and halted there. I already knew nearly all the officers, and they all wanted to know what I thought of Chukus. We sat round the fires for some time laughing and joking and then all went on to within a few miles of Elbasan. I thought we were going to camp there, but we still had another five or six miles' march to the outskirts of Elbasan. Since I had joined this company we had had a day's fighting, then a twelve-hour march, starting at 3 a.m. with a climb to the top of Chukus thrown in, 36 hours' pelting rain, two days' continuous fighting, nothing but a few cobs to eat, and now had been marching since 9 o'clock the night before, yet as we turned at 5 o'clock in the afternoon into the swampy field where we were to camp they had enough spirit left to respond to their company commander's appeal, "Now then, men, left, right, left, right; pull yourselves together and remember you are soldiers," and this was only a sample of what they had been doing for weeks past.

CHAPTER 7

Elbasan—We Push on Towards the Coast

Next day we had a whole blessed day's rest, and the men lay about and rested, and everybody washed their shirts and generally polished themselves up to the best of their ability. Our camp was in a bare and very muddy field about two miles outside Elbasan. In the afternoon Lieut. Jovitch got leave and took me with him to Elbasan to see the sights and show me what an Albanian town is like. It was a filthy little town; the streets paved with big cobble stones and running rivers of mud. The inhabitants were as hostile as they dared to be, and used to refuse to sell us anything. They put the price of bread up to *Frs.* 16 a loaf, and everything else in proportion, and would not sell us any hay for our horses, although they had plenty. Although the men were not allowed into the town then for fear of trouble, they would never forget it, and promised themselves to get some of their own back whenever they came back that way again.

Many of the inhabitants were wearing Austrian overcoats which they had got in exchange for a small piece of bread from the starving Austrian prisoners who passed through there. Some of our men had been given new boots, and, while refusing to sell us anything, the Albanians would try to tempt them by offering a small loaf in exchange for them, and naturally, under the circumstances, they sometimes succeeded.

There was absolutely nothing to see in the town, so we sat for a time in the only Kafana, or hotel, in the place—a dark, dirty little den, with some of the officers whom we met, and drank coffee, and later in the afternoon galloped back as hard as we could to camp through the drenching rain. We found our low-lying field afloat, and the sol-

AN ENGLISH WOMAN-SERGEANT IN SERBIA
THE AUTHOR IN KHAKI

diers had moved to a bit of slightly rising ground where it was not quite so bad. It was raining so hard and everything was so wet that on discovering a sort of loft or small room up a ladder fourteen officers and myself piled in there. Here three of us who had camp beds put them up, and the rest slept on the floor. Of course, as a rule camp beds were no use to us, as you cannot get a camp bed into a bivouac tent. We thought we were going to stay there all night, and would have plenty of time to sleep, and sat about and talked, and some of them played cards all night; so we got a nasty jar when at daylight the order came that we were all to move to another camp. We didn't want any trouble with the natives, but the officers had the men well in hand, and they marched steadily through the town. I rode at the head of our company, while the company commander dropped back alongside and kept his eye on the men; and we all went through without trouble, marching well. We camped in an olive grove beside the river, and most of us went to sleep. It still poured all that day and all night and all the next night and all the next day.

I rode into Elbasan again, and paid a visit to Commandant Militch and his staff, who had taken up quarters in the town. They had arrived that morning, and the rains had been so heavy since we passed that the river had risen and they had had to ford it up to their waists.

We turned out before dawn next morning, and it was horribly cold and damp; we had been sleeping on the wet ground, there being no hay for the horses to eat, and much less for us to sleep on. We had to cross a beautiful old bridge over the wide Schkumba River, and there was a good deal of delay and waiting about. The river had risen, and the bridge did not reach quite far enough, so the men had to cross a plank at the other end, and it took ages for the whole regiment to get across. Those who were on horseback forded the river, which was not very deep, though very wide, with a very rapid current. The fields at the other side were a swamp, and the men were up to their knees in mud and water.

My company was told off to take up a position by itself on a range of hills, and we went up there in the afternoon by a very bad steep track, through bushes with very big prickly thorns. The hills were covered with bracken, which we cut down to make beds of, and pitched our tents in a little hollow. We were all by ourselves up there, and had a very quiet four days, as we seemed at last to have shaken off the pursuing Bulgarians, and it seemed sometimes as if everyone had forgotten all about us. We were the only company up there, and were a very funny-looking camp, with the men sitting about resting and repairing their clothes, and washing hanging out on all the bushes; in fact, we said ourselves that we looked more like a travelling gipsies' encampment than the smartest company in the regiment. Christmas Eve was bright and sunny, and in the afternoon we visited an Albanian village. I was an object of great curiosity to the inhabitants, especially the women, and they always asked Lieut. Jovitch whether I was a woman or a soldier, and seemed very much puzzled when he said I was an Englishwoman but a Serbian soldier.

We were sitting outside one cottage talking to a very old man and his wife. Poor old thing, she patted me all over, examining everything I had on with the deepest interest, and finally disappeared into the cottage and came out again with a bowl of sour milk and some awful-looking bread, of which I ate as much as I could, not to hurt her feelings. We had given the old man some money, and I searched my pockets to see if I could find anything the old woman would like, and finally, feeling rather like "Alice in Wonderland" when she "begged the acceptance of this elegant thimble," I presented her with a small pocket mirror. I do not think she had ever seen such a thing before, and gazed into it with the greatest delight though she looked about a hundred and was ugly enough to frighten the devil.

The Serbian Christmas is not till thirteen days later than ours, but we celebrated my English Christmas Eve over the camp fire that night. A plate of beans and dry bread had to take the place of roast beef and plum pudding, but we drank Christmas healths in a small flask of cognac, after which I played "God Save the King" on the violin, and we all stood up and sang it. This violin went into my long, narrow kit bag, which was carried on a pack-horse and had managed to survive its travels, though the damp had not improved its tone. In the middle of this performance a soldier walked up from the town with the news that the Allies were advancing and that Scoplyé had been retaken by the French, and we were all fearfully bucked. The men came crowding up to hear the news, and immediately began making great plans of turning round and marching straight back into Serbia the way we had come, and we sat round the fire until late, playing and singing to celebrate the victory.

This news afterwards proved to be incorrect, but we quite believed it at the time. We hardly ever did get any news of the outside world and the doings of one's own particular regiment, and more especially the varying fortunes of one's own particular company, seemed to be

SERBIAN SOLDIERS. A COLD CAMP

ROUND THE CAMP FIRE

the most important things in the whole war to us, and what may have been passing during that time on other and more important fronts I did not hear from any reliable source until we got to Durazzo, and not very much then. The greater part of the Serbian Army who went by the northern route through Montenegro to Scutari I heard afterwards had an infinitely worse time than we did, but we did not hear the tale of their sufferings until later, and much has already been written about them.

The next day was Christmas Day, and a Serbian journalist who had spent a great many years in America walked some miles over from his own company to wish me a "Merry Christmas," so that I should hear the old greeting from someone in English.

We had quite settled down to our gipsy life, but the food question had become a serious problem by now; bread was at famine prices, the men had finished all their corn cobs and had had practically nothing to eat for two days. I asked the company commander if it would be possible to buy anything for them, and we sent down into the town and bought a sort of corn meal for *Frs*. 200, and had it baked into flat loaves there in the town, and next day when we turned out for a fresh start we gave each man in the company half of one of my corn meal loaves and a couple of cigarettes, telling them it was England's Christmas box to them, which they ate as they went along, otherwise they would have had to march all that day on nothing. As the other companies who had not been so fortunate saw our men go past munching the last of their corn meal bread they called, "Well done. Fourth Company!" after us, and wanted to join us.

For the first time since we had left Baboona we had shaken off the Bulgarians and were no longer within sound of the guns, but we had to press on or the men would starve.

We had lost hundreds of horses from exhaustion and starvation—once they fell they were too weak to rise again—and their corpses lined the road, or rather track. Sick or well, the men had to keep on. No one could be carried, and you had got to keep on going or die by the roadside.

The next four or five days we continued steadily on our way towards Durazzo, starting about 4 a.m. and generally turning into camp between 6 and 7, long after the short winter afternoons had closed in, so that we had to find our way round our new camping ground in the dark. The weather had got considerably warmer, although the nights were still bitterly cold, and quite a scorching sun used to come out for a few hours in the middle of the day, and this took it out of the tired men a good deal. Before, when I had been working in the hospitals, and I used to ask the men where it hurt them, I had often been rather puzzled at the general reply of the new arrivals, "*Sve me boli*" ("Everything hurts me"), it seemed such a vague description and such a curious malady; but in these days I learnt to understand perfectly what they meant by it, when you seem to be nothing but one pain from the crown of your aching head to the soles of your blistered feet, and I thought it was a very good thing that the next time I was working in a military hospital I should be able to enter into my patient's feelings, and realise that all he felt he wanted was to be let alone to sleep for about a week and only rouse up for his meals.

We went slowly and halted every few hours, sometimes just for a quarter of an hour, sometimes for a good deal longer, and the moment the halt was called everyone used to just drop down on the ground and fall asleep till our company commander would call, "Now then, men, get up," and we would all pull ourselves together, everyone rising immediately without the slightest delay. In the long midday halt we used to join up with the others, and the whole regiment would rest together, and exchange any scraps of news going.

In the evenings the men used to sit round the fires and gossip, and everything that everybody did or said was discussed all through the regiment. News always travels like this among Serbians, and I have often been astonished after I had been away from camp to be told the following day exactly where I had been, whom I had been with, and what I had done. I remember once in Kragujewatz when there were some English officers up in Belgrade who fondly imagined that both their presence and their doings there were a dead secret, in the same curious way we, in the centre of Serbia, knew all about them.

Our riding horses were some of them so starved and exhausted that we could hardly keep the poor brutes on their feet, and I used to sometimes walk to give mine a rest; but at the same time I should have felt more sympathy with it if it had not had a most irritating habit of refusing to stand still for a moment, but kept wheeling round and round in circles. It was a rough mountain pony belonging to my company commander, who, when I joined his company, of course, produced a "reserve" pony for me. The poor little brute died two days after we got to Durazzo.

One night we halted on rather funny camping ground, on the side of a hill covered with holly bushes, and had to find our way through them in the dark. We slept round the fires, as there was not room to put up tents among the prickly bushes. Our company commander, telling his ordnance that they were all too slow for a funeral, lit our fire himself in two minutes under the shelter of a huge holly bush, and we were halfway through supper, very comfortably sitting round a roaring blaze, while other people were still looking for a good spot for their fire, and were asleep at opposite sides of ours before half the others were well alight.

At last we were nearing our journey's end; it was the last day's march, and an unusually long one, too. We passed a company of Italian soldiers, and some of the officers came up early in the morning and visited our camp. Durazzo was being bombarded from the sea, and we could hear the boom of the big naval guns in the distance, but it was all over before we arrived. We marched that day from 5 a.m., which meant, of course, being up at least an hour before, to 8 p.m., with only very short and infrequent halts.

About dusk we reached Kavaia, and all the inhabitants turned out and lined the streets to watch us go past. There, again, they put up everything to famine prices, a tiny flask of cognac which we bought costing *Frs.* 6, in addition to which they would only give us three Italian francs for our Serbian 10-*franc* note.

I never saw anything like the mud in Kavaia; in the town it was a liquid black mass, through which men waded far above their knees, and on the long road between Kavaia and our camping ground it was like treacle. It came right above the tops of my top boots, and one could hardly drag one's feet out of it. The road was full of rocks and pits, and every two or three yards there were dead and dying horses which had floundered down to rise no more; and it was pitch dark and very cold.

Though not very many miles, it took us nearly three hours to do this bit from Kavaia to our camp, there being a block on the road in front of us, and we were absolutely exhausted, when at last we saw the camp fires of the First Company twinkling on the hillside. We kept pushing on and on, and seemed to be never getting any nearer to them; owing to the darkness and the constant blocks caused by the narrow approach to our camp, the road got frightfully congested. I did the latter part of the way on foot, too, and began to wonder if those really were camp fires ahead of us or sort of will-o'-the-wisps getting farther away. At last we turned on to the hillside by the sea, which was to be our resting-place for the next month. I was lying on the grass talking to a soldier, while my orderly put up my tent. He said he was very tired, and I said we all were, but would soon be able to turn in. "Yes," he said thoughtfully, not complaining at all, but merely stating a fact, "but you have ridden most of the way and I have walked, and presently you will have *something* to eat, and I shan't."

There was no supper waiting for the tired man. In the Austrian Army I hear the officers live in luxury while their men starve, but that could most certainly not be said of our officers—beans and bread, and not too much of either, and we had bought the bread ourselves. He was stoking up the fire a little later on, and I called him over and gave him my piece of bread. He shook his head and refused to take it at first, saying, "No, you'll need that yourself," and not till I had quite convinced him that I had enough without it would he take it. We all turned in dead to the world that night, but very glad to have at last reached the coast, and I completely forgot that it was New Year's Eve, though certainly even had I remembered I should not have sat up to see the New Year in.

CHAPTER 8

Serbian Christmas Day at Durazzo

Next day was New Year's Day, and everyone came up and wished me a Happy New Year, our English New Year, that is, as theirs, of course, did not come till thirteen days later, and we all hoped that the New Year might prove happier than the old one had been.

The whole regiment moved their tents up on to the hill and got ship-shape, which, of course, we had not attempted to do in the dark last night. All the men hurried up to the top of the hill to have their first look at the sea, most of them never having seen it before, and they seemed never tired of lying gazing at it. The sea looked quite close, but in reality there was a river and a wide swamp between us and it, as I found to my cost one day when I tried to go down there to bathe. It was lovely weather, and that afternoon the band played for the first time, and we all sat about, or paid visits to each other's tents, and congratulated ourselves that we seemed to be nearing the end of our troubles, though as a matter of fact many poor fellows who had struggled on bravely through Albania succumbed in Durazzo, and thousands more later on in Corfu from the effects of starvation and exposure.

We were about 10 miles from the town of Durazzo, though it did not look anything like so far, and we could see it plainly at the end of the long line of yellow sands jutting out into the sea. There were several wrecks round there, one of them a Greek steamer, which had hit a floating mine. There were a great many of these floating mines about, and the Austrian submarines were also very active, adding immensely to the difficulty of getting food and supplies, which all had to be brought by sea to the troops.

A couple of days after I rode into Durazzo with three of the officers to see the sights of the town. The first sight I did see was a real live English sergeant-major walking down the street. I could hardly believe my eyes, it seemed so long since I had seen an Englishman, and I did not know there were any there. I almost fell on his neck in my excitement, and he seemed equally astonished and pleased to see a fellow countrywoman. He took me up at once to the headquarters of the British Adriatic Mission, and fed me on tea and cakes, while we were waiting for Colonel —— to come in. The same man was also afterwards, strange to say, the first man I met in Salonica, as he was acting as captain of the tug which came to take us off the French steamer on which we had come from Corfu. Afterwards I had lunch with Colonel —— and his staff.

It was the first time for so long that I had sat on a chair and eaten my meals off a table with a table-cloth that I had almost forgotten how to do it. I went back late in the afternoon laden with sundry luxuries they had given me in the way of butter, jam, and a tinned plum pudding, and also two loaves of bread which I had bought in the town, as in those days when we got near a shop we always bought a loaf of bread, in the same way that people at home would buy cake.

I rode back with an artillery officer, who invited me to lunch next day, the other side of Kavaia, and I promised I would come if I could borrow a better horse than the one I was then riding. The road from our camp to Durazzo was in a shocking condition, and it was very hard to ride along it after dark; there were so many dead horses strewn all along it that it was a wonder they did not breed a pestilence.

On my way to my luncheon party next day I met my old friend whose "Slava day" we had celebrated on the top of Mount Kalabac, and stopped there for supper coming back. We had supper by the camp fire with an orchestra of two Tziganes, who sang and played the Serbian airs on their violins. These Tziganes are all very musical and would sooner part with anything than their violin. Some of them play very well, and they can do a very difficult thing—sing a song and play their own accompaniment with chords on the violin at the same time.

The next day, the men having by now had a little time to get rested, there was a big parade and inspection, though we were a somewhat ragged-looking regiment for a full-dress parade.

On the Serbian Christmas Eve there was a great ceremony, which is always kept up. Of course, we only kept it on a small scale, but I was told that in Belgrade in peace time it was a very splendid affair indeed. This was cutting the Christmas oak. All the officers rode out to a wood, where the band played, and there was a sort of service conducted by the priest, and then we came back carrying a small oak tree, and there were refreshments and much drinking of healths.

We kept up Christmas festivities for three days, and the men had extra rations, and all had roast pig, which even the very poorest family in Serbia always has on Christmas Day. In the evening I was invited to dinner with the colonel of the regiment and his staff; we drank the healths of England and Serbia together, and kept it up till very late. They put a gold coin in their pudding like we put things in our English plum puddings, and I got the slice containing it. They told me it was very lucky, and I always wear it now. On Christmas Eve they roast nuts like we do on Twelfth Night. It is the same date as our Twelfth Night, and I was surprised to find that they had many of these old customs which are now found more in Ireland than in England. Although they did their best to make a bluff at having a happy Christmas it was a very sad and homesick one for them really, not knowing in the least where their families were spending theirs, or if they would ever meet again.

We had fixed ourselves up pretty comfortably by now. By digging out a place about 2 ft. deep, building up the earth into a wall all round and pitching the tent on to the top of that you can turn a small bivouac tent into quite a large and commodious abode, which will contain a camp bed if you have one and a fireplace with an earth chimney for the smoke, and when you have a fire going and four or five of you are sitting in there no one need complain of the cold, even on the coldest evening; and the evenings were still very cold indeed, although the days were hot. I used to ride into Durazzo fairly often to see my English friends there, who were more than kind and hospitable to me, and used to give me many little luxuries to take back with which to eke out our slender rations, as, no longer having the hard exercise every day to put an edge on our appetites, we seemed rather to have turned against beans. Though a corporal, I always messed with the officers.

The British Adriatic Mission were feeding the Serbian Army, and were doing wonders, though owing to the constant arrival of fresh troops and the scarcity of ovens for baking their bread (although they were building fresh ones as fast as ever they could) the men were still on half rations of bread, and some days had to have biscuits instead; but, of course, the men could have eaten a lot more after their months of starvation. Among other things they had had some coffee given to them, but it was not much use, as they had no sugar, and the kindly inhabitants of Durazzo had made a corner in sugar and put the price up to *Frs.* 16 a kilo; so it was impossible to buy it for them, and I racked my brains as to how I could get some at least for my own company. I asked the head of the B.A.M., but he, of course, could not make an exception of one particular company, even if it had an English corporal (I had been made corporal on New Year's Day, and promoted sergeant three months later), but he said he would see what could be done and turned the matter over to his adjutant. He, being a young man of resource, went to a Red Cross organisation and demanded a *year's rations* of sugar for an English nurse.

I do not know what the daily ration of sugar for an English nurse may be, but, anyhow, one year's worked out at a good-sized case, which I brought back in triumph (having borrowed a packhorse in Durazzo for that purpose) and divided up amongst my company, and perfect peace reigned in the camp, the men all spending a very happy afternoon sitting round their little camp fires, making endless little cups of sweet black Turkish coffee. I hope the American Red Cross will forgive me for sharing my year's rations with belligerents if they should ever chance to read this.

I got myself into sad disgrace one day, however, by going away from the camp without leave. An officer from another battalion was going to lunch at another camp some miles away, and he invited me to ride over with him. We started very early in the morning, and, as I could not find the commander of my company to ask leave, I just went. We stayed there, not only for lunch, but for supper and all the evening as well, and I would not like to say what time it was when we got back. The next morning my company commander pointed out to me one of the soldiers up on the hillside doing four hours' punishment drill, standing up there with his rifle, accoutrements and heavy pack in the hot sun, and I was told that on this occasion I should be let off with a reprimand (although I had been three months in the army and ought to know better by this time), but if I did not see the error of my ways I should find myself doing something similar to that next time, or five days' C.B. I got my revenge, however, a few days later, when he fell sick, and I returned to my original vocation of nurse. He was a very docile patient for a week, though after that he suddenly thought it was time to reassert his authority, so got up one day when my back was turned, and ate everything I had not allowed him to eat while in bed.

I had a telegram one day from Durazzo from my friend Miss Sim-

SERBIAN SOLDIERS IN THEIR OWN SERBIAN UNIFORMS,
BEFORE GETTING ENGLISH KHAKI

monds, telling me to come and meet her in Durazzo at once. She and I had worked together in the Serbian hospitals ever since the beginning of the war, and as soon as she got my letter saying I was starting back for Serbia she had left New York to join me again, but, of course, could not find me, as by the time she got to Salonica I had disappeared into Albania. She had been doing most wonderful work ever since, organising relief for Serbian refugees and personally conducting shiploads of them from Salonica to Corsica, Marseilles and goodness knows where. Among other little odd jobs she discovered a whole colony of them in Brindisi who had been without food for two days; so without any further red tape proceeded to hire carriages, drive round the town and buy up everything in the eatable line which was to be had wherewith to feed them.

I at once borrowed a horse and rode out to Durazzo to meet her. I did not know in the least where to find her there, but most of the people in the town seemed to have heard of her, and I finally located her at the Serbian crown prince's house, where she had gone to be presented. He was not going to see any more people that day, but when he heard that I had arrived he very kindly said that he would see me too. I was not exactly dressed to be presented to royalty, as I was still wearing the clothes (the only ones I had) in which I had come through Albania, besides having just had a hot and dusty 10 mile ride, but that doesn't matter in wartime. He was most charming, and decorated us both with the *Sveti Sava* medal.

After that we went on board her ship, in which she was sailing that night with 1,500 refugees which she was taking to Corsica. We had a busy evening, and had our work cut out for us feeding 1,500 refugees on bully beef and biscuits. The ship, which was a small Greek one, was simply packed, and it was no easy task on the pitch dark decks and down in the holds.

I slept in town that night. One of the English officers was waiting on the quay for me when I got back at midnight, and he had found me room in an hotel. The hotels in Durazzo are the limit, but this one did at a pinch. He asked the boy in the hotel if he could make us some tea. He said he could as far as the boiling water went, but he had neither tea nor sugar. A Serbian officer, a stranger to us both, who happened to be passing on his way to bed, overheard this, and immediately said he had both tea and sugar, which he would give us; and not only did he do this, but came back afterwards and apologised for not having any cognac to put into it. As my friend remarked, "Really the Serbians do give us points in the way of manners; here is a man who, not satisfied with seeing to the comfort of two people who are total strangers to him, and providing them with his own tea and sugar, comes back and actually apologises because he has not cognac as well!"

The next morning I went round to the British Adriatic Mission, and while I was having breakfast there there was a most terrific crash, followed by others in quick succession. I left my breakfast and went out into the street to see what was to be seen. Five Austrian aeroplanes were circling round and round overhead, apparently dropping bombs as fast as they could. The streets of Durazzo are very, very narrow, and the town is very small and very crowded. People were running as hard as they could to get out of the way—at least, the Italians were running, the Serbians always thought it beneath their dignity to do so. I was standing with a Serbian artillery officer who knew all about it and could almost always guess pretty well where they were going to fall. Looking up into the clear blue sky you could see the bombs quite well as they left the aeroplanes: first of all they looked like a silvery streak of light, and then like a thin streak of mist falling through the sky, till they hit some building with a crash, smothering everyone in the neighbourhood with a powdery white dust.

Two of them fell in almost identically the same spot at the end of the street about a hundred yards from us, and several more round about. Another officer joined us presently who was very much annoyed because he was in the middle of being shaved when the first bomb fell, and the Italian barber had, without more ado, instantly dropped his razor and fled, so that he had to come out with only half his face shaved. He was rather glad afterwards, however, when he found out that had the barber remained he would have had no face left to shave, as when we walked back to the shop we found that a bomb had gone clean through the roof and the barber was standing outside anathematising aeroplanes for ruining his business. Altogether they dropped twenty-five bombs in about a quarter of an hour within a radius of a little over a quarter of a mile and killed a good many people.

There was a wide subterranean drain leading from the town to the sea, and down this hundreds of Italians crawled, but I think if I were given the choice of crawling down a Durazzo drain in close proximity to some hundreds of the natives of that town or being killed by a bomb I would choose the latter. One day previously some bombs had fallen in the neighbourhood of a camp of Italian soldiers, who had to vacate it. A company of hungry Serbians near by had with great presence of mind seized the opportunity to go in and clear the deserted camp of all the bread and everything eatable it contained, and they were heard to express a wish afterwards that there might be a visitation of aeroplanes every day. When it was all over I went back again, and, finding the headquarters of the British Adriatic Mission still standing, sat down to a fresh lot of bacon and eggs for breakfast, such luxuries not being obtainable every day.

CHAPTER 9

We Go to Corfu

We remained near Durazzo for a month, the men resting and re-
cuperating after their hard time.

There were a lot of young recruits who had been brought through
with the army from Serbia, but who had not yet been formally sworn
in, and one morning this ceremony took place. The whole regiment
was formed up in a square in the centre of which stood the priest with
a table in front of him, on which were a bowl of holy water, with a
bunch of leaves beside it, a Serbian Bible, and a large brass cross. All the
officers were drawn up in a double line facing the table, and the recruits behind them again, with the whole regiment forming the other
two sides of the square and the band a little way behind.

The priest read a sort of short service, and then the flag-bearer carried the regimental flag up to the table while the band played. After
that the priest walked all down the line of officers with the basin of
holy water in his hand, and dipping the bunch of leaves into it sprin-
kled them each on the forehead and held up the cross for them to kiss;
when that was over the swearing in of the new recruits began, and,
as I had not yet been sworn in, I was one of them. We all stood at the
salute and repeated the oath all together, sentence by sentence after
the priest, swearing loyalty to Serbia and King Peter, and after that we
marched in single file past the table, removing our caps as we did so
for the priest to sprinkle our foreheads, and then kissed the cross, the
priest's hand, and, last of all, the regimental flag. It was a very impres-
sive ceremony, winding up by the band playing the Serbian National
Anthem while we stood at the salute.

All the officers came up and shook hands with me afterwards and
congratulated me on now being properly enrolled as a soldier in the

Serbian Army.

We were getting very tired of the Adriatic coast, and now that we were feeling rested again we were anxious to be once more on the move and take the next step towards getting back to Serbia. Speculation was rife as to where we were going to be sent to be reorganised and refitted; no one knew for certain, and there were the wildest rumours about Algiers, France, or Alexandria, but at last the glad news came that we were really going, and to Corfu.

But there was still a six or seven days' march to Vallona, where the regiment was to embark. Doctors came round and every man was medically examined to see if he was fit for the march, as those who were not were to be embarked at Durazzo. We had heard that the road to Vallona was very bad, and in some places knee-deep in mud and water, and nobody was very anxious for the march if he could go from Durazzo, so one and all declared that they had rheumatism or else sore feet; but eventually only a small percentage, among them sixty men from the Fourth Company, and about half a dozen officers, from the regiment were declared to be unfit. I was perfectly fit, but, as I was told I might do whichever I liked, I thought I might as well embark at Durazzo with those from my own company; so on the 3rd of February we left our camp and went into Durazzo to wait for the steamer, as it was uncertain which day she would sail.

I and some of the officers who were not on duty took rooms in the town, and there we had to wait for four days. We found some difficulty in feeding ourselves; there seemed to be hardly anything to buy, and what there was was at famine prices, and our Serbian 10-*franc* notes were only worth three and a half Greek or Italian *francs*. We had to pay 50 *francs* for a bottle of common red wine, which anywhere else would have cost a *franc*. One day some Italian doctors invited us to lunch at their hospital; they were most excellent hosts, and it was a very large and merry luncheon party. Hardly any two people could talk the same language, and English, French, German, Spanish, Italian and Serbian got all mixed up together into a sort of Esperanto of our own.

Every day as regularly as clockwork, between half-past ten and eleven, we had an Austrian aeroplane raid, and occasionally in the afternoon as well, and we got so used to them that if we did not hear the first bomb in time we used to gaze up into the sky and wonder why they were so late, but the worst raid was when we were actually embarking.

Embarking is always a tedious business, and is always inseparably connected in my mind with hours of standing about on your own weary feet, like a flock of tired sheep, in weather that is always either too hot or too cold, or else raining, patiently waiting for orders.

We were embarked on large flat barges, and sent off to two or three small Italian steamers in the harbour. The one that I was on was crammed with men, and we had just got alongside the steamer when an aeroplane came exactly overhead. We made a fairly big mark with the large crowded barge alongside the steamer, and it passed over us three times, dropping bombs all around as if they were shelling peas. Backwards and forwards it came, columns of water shooting up, now 50 yards to the right, now a little to the left, showing where the bombs hit the water harmlessly, one of them barely clearing a hospital ship at anchor. Every moment it seemed as if the next one must drop in the middle of our barge, but we were pretty well seasoned to anything by now, and, whatever may have been our inside feelings, we sat still and stolidly watched sudden death hovering over our heads in the blue sky, but it didn't seem somehow like playing the game when we couldn't retaliate at all. The captain of the Italian steamer got so exasperated that he shouted that he was not going to have his steamer sunk on our account, and that we were to sheer off, as he would not take us on board at all; so our tug towed us back to the pier for further orders, and we were eventually sent off to another steamer.

I and the two officers I was with in the end found ourselves embarked on one steamer, with most of the men from our own regiment on another, and our servants and all our luggage on a third. By that time it was about 1 o'clock, and, as we had been standing about in the hot sun since 5 a.m. and had had nothing to eat, we began to feel as if we should like some breakfast; so we were any thing but pleased to be told upon enquiry that nobody could get anything to eat on that ship, neither officers nor men.

"Now then, Corporal," said my company commander to me," you talk French; go and see what you can do." So I obediently went off to hunt up the military commander of the ship. He first informed me that there was no food on the boat, and that nobody could get anything until 8 o'clock that evening, and seemed to be inclined to let the matter go at that, but I was not going to take that answer back if I could help it; so told him that I didn't think much of his way of treating his English Allies, whereupon, having turned that over in his mind, he said I could have something alone. Of course that was no use;

so after a little more persuasion I finally got him to order the steward to serve dinner to the two officers and myself in the saloon in about an hour as soon as it could be got ready, and while waiting for it we could have some coffee, if I could get anybody to make it for me. I accordingly went round to the galley and interviewed the cook, who informed me that the man who made the coffee was asleep in his bunk and I couldn't wake him.

"Oh, can't I?" I said (in the words of the man when told by the steward that he could not be sick in the saloon), "you'll see if I can't."

"Are you an officer?" he inquired, with that sort of veiled impertinence that the lower class Italians and Greeks are such past-masters of.

"No, I am not," I snapped, "I am a corporal; now which is that coffee-man's cabin?" and, on it being pointed out to me, I beat such a devil's tattoo on the door with my riding-whip that in half a minute a very tousled and sleepy head appeared, and enquired what on earth was the matter. I told him I wanted three cups of coffee in the saloon *at once*, and he was so astonished that he got up forthwith and made them, and I went back in triumph to report, and felt rewarded on being told that I had done very well.

The next morning we were transferred in Vallona harbour on to a big Italian steamer, a fine boat, where they treated us very well. We reached Corfu about 1 a.m., and disembarking began there and then. We hung on till the last, as we had nowhere to spend the night, our tents, blankets, etc., being on another boat, and I had not even an overcoat with me and it was very cold, but at 3 a.m. we also had to go.

We had been looking forward to Corfu as a sort of land flowing with milk and honey, with a magnificent climate and everything that was good, but our ardour was rather damped when we landed at that hour at a small quay, feet deep in mud, miles away from the town, and about 8 miles away from our camp, so we were told. We did not know in which direction our camp was, and, even had we got there, would have been no better off without a tent or blankets; so we spent the remainder of the night sitting on a packing-case beside the sentry's fire, and I was glad enough to be able to borrow an overcoat from the Serbian officer in charge of the quay, who was just going off duty.

There was one of the most beautiful sunrises I have ever seen, but under some circumstances you feel you would most willingly barter the most gorgeous panorama of scenery for a cup of hot tea.

We had a long, hot walk the next morning till we found our own division, where the sixty men from our company were camped pending the arrival of the commandant of the regiment and the rest who were coming *via*Vallona.

Corfu may be a lovely climate and a health resort and everything else that is delightful at any other time in the year, but it was a bitter blow to us when it rained for about six weeks without stopping after our arrival, added to which there was no wood, and camp fires were forbidden, I suppose for fear that the men might take to cutting down the olive trees with which the island is covered. There was no hay at first for us to sleep on, and the incessant wet, combined with the effects of bully beef, on men whose stomachs were absolutely destroyed by months of semi-starvation was largely responsible for the terrible amount of sickness and very high mortality among the troops during the first month of our stay there. This was especially the case among the boys and young recruits, who, less hardy than the trained soldiers, were completely broken down by their late hardships and died by thousands on the hospital island of Vido.

They could not be buried in the small island, dying as they were at the rate of 150 a day, and the bodies were taken out to sea. The Serbs are not a maritime nation, and the idea of a burial at sea is repugnant to them. I heard one touching story. An old man came to the island to see his son, but he had died the day before. "Where is his grave?" he asked, "that I may tell my old wife I saw his last resting-place. We had seven sons; six were killed in the war, and he was the seventh and youngest." The kind-hearted doctor lied bravely and well. "That is it," he said, pointing to a little wooden cross among a few others, where some graves had been made one day when it was too rough for the tug to call. How could he tell the poor old father that even then his son's body was lying out on the wooden jetty waiting to be carried out to his nameless grave in the blue Ionian Sea?

We found there had been some hitch in the commissariat arrangements, and there was no food for our sixty men. We bought them some bread next day, but bread was 3 *francs* a loaf, and a third of a loaf to a man with nothing else was not enough to keep them going, while endless red tape was being unwound before their proper rations came along. They never made a complaint; but, though we could have bought bread for ourselves, it nearly choked us with the men standing round silently watching and wondering what we were going to do for them.

On the second morning, seeing an empty motor-lorry coming along, I had a sudden inspiration and boarded it, dashing down the steep bank to the road, telling them that I would be back in the evening from town with something for them, and taking an orderly with me. It was about fifteen miles' drive into the town of Corfu, and I tramped about all day in the pouring rain from one official to another, from the English to the French, from the French to the Serbians, and back again to the French, till I was heartily sick of it, and had I had the money would have bought the stuff in the town and had done with it. There was plenty of bread at the bakery, but, of course, they could not give it to me without a proper requisition, which apparently I could not sign because I was not authorised to do so.

It was getting towards evening, and I was beginning to despair, and was thinking of doing the best I could with a hundred *francs* I had borrowed, when I thought I would have one more try with the French authorities. I was wet through myself, as I had had no time to stop for a coat when the lorry came along, and had been too busy and too worried to get anything to eat all day, but anyhow this time I managed to pitch them such a pitiful tale of woe about the sufferings of the men, and the awful time I was having trying to get them something to eat, that I quite softened their hearts, and they said they would give me what I wanted without any further signature, but that I must not make a precedent of this unofficial way of doing business.

I was overjoyed, and sent my orderly off at once to hunt up a carriage, and we returned to camp in triumph about 9 o'clock with a whole sackful of bread, another of tinned beef, and two large earthenware jars of wine, which I bought on the way. There were plenty of the men waiting, when they heard my carriage arrive, to dash down to the road and carry the stuff up to the camp, and there was great rejoicing over the success of my expedition. I was soon warm and dry and having some supper myself. The men were all right so far, but another day's short rations would certainly have seen some of them sick.

The question of transport was fearfully difficult, and the French and English authorities were working night and day to feed the troops, and, of course, they could never have got through the work if things had not been done in order; so I was duly grateful that under the special circumstances they let me carry out such an unauthorised raid.

About a week later the rest of the company arrived about 10 o'clock one evening, and a sergeant proudly told me that our Fourth Company were all very fit and not a man sick or fallen out.

We moved to another camp up in the hills, a nice place, but very far from anywhere, though I found that I could get about anywhere I wanted to on the motor-lorries which used to come in with bread. The A.S.C. drivers of these lorries must have had a hard time at first; the roads were very bad and the weather shocking, and they were working sixteen hours a day carrying supplies, but they were full of pity for the deplorable condition of the Serbian soldiers, and were willingly working night and day to alleviate it.

One of the English officers gave me a small Italian tent in place of the little Serbian bivouac one I had been sleeping in. It was a capital little tent, very light and absolutely waterproof. My orderly built a foundation of stones about 2 ft. high, with the chinks filled in with earth, and pitched the tent on the top of that, so that it was quite high enough to stand up in and also to hold a camp bed and a rubber bath, and he then made a nice little garden and planted it with shrubs and flowers, with a little wall all round ornamented with red bully-beef tins with plants in them, and it looked awfully nice.

The thing we missed most was not being able to have any fires to sit round. One day I came back on a lorry containing a load of wood intended for somewhere else, but I had got past any scruples about commandeering anything where my own company was concerned; so I persuaded the driver to drop a few big logs off on the road at the nearest point to our camp, and we had at least one small fire for some time afterwards, and anybody who liked could come and boil his billy-can and make his tea at that.

The Serbian Relief Fund was shorthanded and very busy, and I obtained permission to leave the camp for a few weeks and take up my quarters in town to give them a hand. Several shiploads of stuff had just come in, and everything had to be landed on the quay on lighters and then removed from there at once, as the quay could not be blocked up, to one or other of their two store-houses, which were at opposite ends of the harbour. One of these store-houses had only just been acquired, and, as it was about 6 in. deep in coal dust, it had all to be scrubbed and cleaned out for the arrival of fresh bales, and that was my first job. I got a gang of Serbian soldiers, and we had a strenuous day's work with the very inefficient tools at our disposal, but we managed by the evening to get everything ship-shape and the floors clean, though we all got rather damp and coal-dusty in the process.

The quay was a most interesting place, though I should have enjoyed the work more if it had not poured steadily all day and every day, as there was no cover anywhere. French, English, and Serbians were all working there together, each trying to be the first to seize upon labour and transport both by water and land for the particular job he was responsible for. There were a number of ships in the harbour waiting to be unloaded, and everyone was working as hard as he could, and things were considerably complicated by the fact that hardly one of them could speak the other's language. It was quite a usual thing to find an Englishman, who could not speak French, trying to explain to a French official that he wanted a fatigue party of Serbian soldiers to unload a certain lighter, and neither of them being able to explain to the said fatigue party, when they had got them, what it was they wanted them to do.

There was always a company of Serbian soldiers for work on the quay, and a fresh relay of men came on at 6 a.m., at midday, and at 6 p.m., and you had to be there sharp on time if you wanted your men, or else you would find they had all been snapped up by someone else. As I could speak French and enough Serbian to get along very well, most of my work was on the quay, and I was often called in to act as interpreter. As I did not want to get down there at 6 a.m., however, I got a friendly English corporal, who had to be on duty then, to get twice as many men as he wanted himself, and then give me half of them when I came down. I was rather afraid of the English Tommies at first, and thought they would be sure to laugh at a woman corporal, but, on the contrary, there was nothing they would not do to help me, and the French soldiers were just the same.

I was superintending the unloading of some goods from a lighter one day, which all had to be transferred to another lighter, and taken across to the warehouse that evening. We were all very tired and wet, and the men were slacking off, and it didn't seem, at the rate we were going on, as if we should get through before 9 or 10 o'clock that night. The Serbian sergeant tried to buck them up, but the men were fed up and were just doing about as little as they possibly could. It is worse than useless to bully a Serbian soldier if he doesn't want to do anything; so, as I wanted to get back to the hotel to dinner, I went on quite another tack. I told them I had been working for them all day since early in the morning, and was tired and hungry, and that if they were going to spend another three hours over the job I should get no dinner. The effect was magical. They all at once got terribly worried on my account, began to work like steam, and in an hour we had the whole thing done, and they were enquiring in a brotherly manner if it was all right, and if I would be in time for dinner now.

All these poor fellows working down on the quay had had their uniforms taken away from them and burnt, and had been provided with a blue corduroy suit for working in. Their old ones, though dirty, were warm, and their new ones were very thin, and in most cases they had hardly any underclothes; so whenever I had a gang of men working under me down at the warehouse I used to fit them out with warm sweaters, etc., of which we had plenty, out of one of the broken bales. I used to make them work hard for a couple of hours, and then sit down for five minutes and have a cigarette, and then go on again for another hard spell. The Serbian sergeants used to be very much amused at my methods, but I always found they answered very well. They were always keen to be on my gang, and everyone said I got more work out of them than anyone else could.

There were a lot of new English uniforms, but the French authorities would not issue them unless there were enough underclothes to go with them, and these they were short of. However, I got a promise of underclothes from the Serbian Relief Fund, and then my troubles began. First I had to get a paper signed by the English saying they would give them if the French approved; then another, signed by the French, that they did approve and would give the uniforms; then one signed by the Serbian Minister of War; then back to the French again to be countersigned; then back to the Minister of War; then to the Serbian warehouse, who refused to give them because I hadn't got somebody else's signature, and so on and so on. To cut a long story short, it took three whole days walking round Corfu in the pouring rain before I could get all those papers sufficiently signed, including three visits to the Minister of War, and even then the transport remained to be found, as the motor-lorries were fully occupied carrying bread.

I had airily promised the French that I thought the English authorities could give me the transport; so I went up to them, and they said they would see what they could do.

"How much stuff have you?" inquired the officer in charge.

"Three thousand two hundred and fifty uniforms," I replied, "and the same number of vests and pants."

"Well, that doesn't tell me anything," he said; "I want to know the bulk and weight: you're no good as a corporal if you can't tell me that. Let me know exactly by eleven o'clock tomorrow morning, and I'll see what I can do."

Here was a poser, for, though I said at once that I would let him

OFFICERS SITTING OUTSIDE MY TENT

COLONEL MILITCH ON DIANA

know, I had not the faintest idea of how to work it out; but fortunately bethought myself of my sheet anchor, the big English corporal on the quay, who always seemed to be able to solve any difficulty; and, sure enough, he did it for me, and I telephoned the required information. In the end I got the stuff loaded on to a barge and took it myself to a point about 2 miles from my camp, whence it was carried up by a company, and we had the proud distinction of being the first regiment to be fitted out in new, clean English khaki uniforms. When not on the quay there was plenty to do in the warehouses, sorting out the bales, or taking them across the harbour in our little tug, which was quite a journey, but I eventually got a chill and had to lay off for a bit, as the result of one wetting too many.

I used to go back to camp every Saturday afternoon and Sunday, and I always managed to take up a couple of cases of something, generally given me by the Serbian Relief Fund; either things for the ambulance or condensed milk or golden syrup for the men. Condensed milk was very much appreciated, as it meant that they each got a big bowl of *café au lait* for breakfast for three mornings, whereas, as a rule, they don't have anything until lunch.

One day an incident occurred which touched me very greatly. The non-commissioned officers and men of the Fourth Company formed a committee among themselves and drew up an address, which they presented me with, and which a man in the regiment who knew English afterwards translated for me as literally as possible. An English major, to whom I once showed it, told me if that were his he should value it more than a whole string of medals, and as that is how I feel about it, coming as it did spontaneously from my own men, I put the translation in here:

To the high-esteemed
Miss Flora Sandes,

Corfu.

Esteemed Miss Sandes!
Soldiers of the Fourth Company, 1st Battalion, 2nd Inf. Rgmt., 'Knjaza Michaila,' Moravian Division, 1st (Call) Reserves; touched with your nobleness, wish with this letter to pay their respects—and thankfulness to you; have chosen a committee to hand to you this letter of thankfulness.
Miss Sandes!
Serbian soldier is proud because in his midst he sees a noble

daughter of England, whose people is an old Serbian friend, and today their armies are arm-in-arm fighting for common idea, and you Miss Sandes should be proud that you are in position to do a good, to help a Serbian soldier—Serbian soldier will always respect acts of your kindness and deep down in his heart will write you kind acts and remember them for ever.

Few months have passed since you came among us, and you shared good and bad with us. During this time you have often helped us to pass through hardships, buying food for us, and financially.

Thanking you in the name of all the soldiers, we are greeting you with exclamation:

Long life to our ally England,
Long life to Serbia,
Long life to their heroic Armies,
Long life to noble Miss Sandes!

Naredniks (SergeantMajors)—
  Milcontije Simitch
  Rangel Miloshevitch

Podnaredniks (Sergeants)—
  Milisav Stamenkovitch
  Yanatchko Todorovitch
  Bozidar Milenkovitch

Kaplars (Corporals)—
  Vladimar Stankovitch
  Milan Jovanovitch
  Dragutin Rangjelovitch
  Aleksa Miloshevitch
  Zaphir Arsitch

Vojnitsi (Soldiers)—
  Milivoye Pavlovitch
  Milorad Taskavitch
  Rangel Mladenovitch
  Dragoljub Milovanovitch
  Alexandar Iwkovitch

4th Comp., 1st Battl., 2nd Inf. Rgt.

No. 1024 (Official Stamp).

To Miss Sandes, Corporal, volunteer of this Comp.—

Please receive this little, but from heart of my soldiers, declaration of thankfulness for all (for help) that you have done for them until now, and in time, when they are far away from dear ones and loving ones at home.

To their wishes and declaration I am adding mine and exclaim:

Long life to our dear ally England,

Long life to heroic Serbian Army,

Commander of the Company,

Janachko A. Jovitch.

13/26 February, 1916.

Ipsos (Corfu).

CHAPTER 10

The "Slava Day" of the Second Regiment

The companies used to take turns at working at the ports for about three weeks, and when our turn came the men were very pleased, as they much preferred it to doing drill, and they were able to occasionally get into the town also. We were camped about a mile and a half outside the town, but I thought it was the nastiest camp that I had ever been in—a very small crowded piece of ground with no shade, so that when the weather was hot we were perfectly roasted, and when it was wet, when you tried to climb up the narrow steep path to it, you slipped back two steps for one you went up, in the thick, slippery mud.

I gave up my room in town, as our camp was close enough to walk to. I could make myself understood pretty well in Serbian by now, though, of course, I made awful mistakes, as it is by far the most difficult language I have ever come across to learn, there being no books to help one. One can only pick it up by ear; so it is no wonder if I was occasionally misunderstood.

One day I told my orderly to go and fetch my thick coat, which he would find on a chair in my room, and bring it to me in camp. He duly arrived back about an hour afterwards with the coat *and* the chair, which he had carried all through the town, and was much discomfited at the howls of laughter with which we all greeted him. I asked him what the landlady had said to his removing her furniture like that, and he confessed that she had made a few remarks, but, as she spoke nothing but Italian and he nothing but Serbian, they passed lightly over his head, and he triumphantly carried out what he had taken to be my orders. He was a capital orderly, always cheerful and

231

willing. One day he told me, in answer to some remark of mine, that as my orderly he would not have to fight. "Will you fight with us going back to Serbia, like you did in Albania?" he asked.

"Why, of course I shall, Dragoutini," I said.

His face beamed. "Then I shall go with you and fight beside you," he declared emphatically.

We went back to our camp in the hills when our three weeks were up, and to our great joy we heard that we were to embark almost immediately for Salonica.

They let us stay a day longer than was intended in order to celebrate the regimental "*Slava* day," which is a great festival, and the whole regiment was *en fête* for the whole day. The Crown Prince Alexander himself came, and a great many French and English officers and a few ladies.

It was held in a beautiful big, flat glade, just below the camp, with huge big spreading trees. There was a large marquee decorated with all the different flags of the Allies, and everybody had been busy for the last week making paths and generally beautifying the place, and practising for the big march past of the regiment.

We had a variety of talent in our regiment; among others a young student of sculpture. Building four high pillars of clayey mud flanking the path leading to the marquee, he carved on each a beautiful bas-relief. The first one represented a haggard, weary, beaten Serbian soldier going into exile; the next a Serbian soldier re-equipped, holding his new rifle in his hand, his expression full of fierce determination, standing in a striking attitude with his face to the foe again; while on a third was the head of a woman with a look of patient expectancy on her beautiful face, representing the women who were waiting in Serbia for the return of their sons and husbands to deliver them from the bondage of the hated Austrian-Bulgarian oppressors. They were most striking figures, and some day that young Serbian soldier will become known as a very great sculptor.

It was an ideal spot for a *fête*, and we hoped anxiously that the weather, which had looked rather threatening, would hold up. The whole regiment was astir very early, and we were all drawn up under the trees before the guests arrived.

I was talking to the colonel, when he suddenly asked me where my company was drawn up.

"Just behind the Third," I replied, pointing over in that direction.

"Well, come over there with me, I want to speak to them," he said, and we went over, I wondering what he was going to say, and was more than astonished when I found the surprise in store for me. They all sprang to attention, and then, with me standing by his side, he made them a long speech, which all the other companies round could hear also, and said that he was promoting me to sergeant on that their great regimental "*Slava* day." Generally you are just promoted, and it is entered in the books in the ordinary way, and it was a very great honour to have a public sort of ceremony like that, especially on such a day. They all shouted "*Jivio*" three times for me when he had finished, and, though I felt extremely shy and embarrassed, I was very much pleased.

All the officers in the regiment and a great many of the men came up and shook hands with me afterwards, and congratulated me, and the commander of the battalion sent his orderly off for some spare stars which he had, and fixed my second ones on my shoulders there and then.

Later on the general of the First Army, who was one of the guests, when he heard I was one of his soldiers, also added his congratulations; in fact, I have never in my life had so much handshaking and patting on the back.

Presently the crown prince arrived and the rest of the guests. The whole regiment, headed by the band and the regimental flag, marched past him and saluted, and to see these fine healthy-looking fellows, with their swinging stride, you would never have guessed they were the same men who had gone through that terrible retreat in the Albanian mountains and arrived at Corfu in such a deplorable condition two months before.

The guests all sat down to lunch in the big marquee, and after that there were songs, dancing, etc. The crown prince had to leave early, but said he would come back again later on.

I had invited two of my friends from the English hospital, and they enjoyed themselves immensely, and we all—guests, officers and men—danced the "*Kolo*" and all the other Serbian national dances together until evening.

Later on there was another big lunch and a great many speeches from the representatives of the English, French and Italian Allies. True to his promise Prince Alexander came back later in the afternoon, specially to chat with the soldiers, among whom he walked about in the friendliest manner, enquiring after their families, how they had been wounded, etc., etc. It was easy to see how popular he is with his army, and how pleased and proud the men were as they crowded round him.

We kept it up the whole day and late that night after all the guests had gone, in spite of the fact that we should have to be astir very early next morning, as we were to embark for Salonica.

We had a very hot, dusty tramp down to the embarking stage, and I had very bad luck, as I lost my dog "Mah," who was a most faithful little brute, though it would be hard to describe his breed. He was a stray who had attached himself to an officer and afterwards been handed over to me, and he was always at my heels, never quitting me for a moment and sleeping in my tent. Even when I was dancing the previous day he had nearly upset several people in his anxiety to keep close to me. It was only about half an hour before the boat sailed that I missed him. In the immense crowd of soldiers he had lost sight of me for a moment, and then could not trace me, and someone eventually told me that they had seen him starting back along the hot, dusty road to camp looking for me, and, as I dared not miss the boat on his account, I had reluctantly to give up the search.

The boat was a fine French Transatlantic boat, but the first day out at sea was very rough, and the men, who are anything but good sailors, lay about prostrate, declaring that they would rather have ten days' continuous battle on land than one day on board ship.

However, Easter Sunday was very fine, and we all landed next day quite fit at Salonica. Our camp was up on the hills about seventeen miles from the town. It was a lovely place, and had the further advantage of having a spring of very good mineral water, which was a great luxury, as the drinking water around Salonica is not good as a rule.

The transportation of the Serbian Army from Corfu to Salonica was going on apace, and within a few weeks the whole force was safely landed without a single casualty.

The men were fully equipped down to the very last button—new English khaki uniforms, belts, rifles, water-bottles, absolutely everything.

I went home on a couple of months' leave, leaving them full of spirits, and eagerly looking forward to the time when we could get another whack at the enemy, and march victoriously back into Serbia; and with any luck I hope some day to be able to describe how we accomplished it, and the triumphal entry into Nish which we are always talking about.

www.ingramcontent.com/pod-product-compliance
Lightning Source LLC
Chambersburg PA
CBHW032049080426
42733CB00006B/213